FAMOUS
BRITISH BATTLES

FAMOUS
BRITISH BATTLES

Geoffrey Regan

MICHAEL O'MARA BOOKS LIMITED

First published in Great Britain in 1997 by
Michael O'Mara Books Limited
9 Lion Yard
Tremadoc Road
London SW4 7NQ

A CIP catalogue record for this book is available
from the British Library

ISBN 1-85479-295-4

1 3 5 7 9 10 8 6 4 2

Designed and typeset by K DESIGN, Winscombe, Somerset
Printed and bound by Clays Ltd, St Ives plc

Contents

Contents

Acknowledgements

The publishers would like to thank the following for their permission to reproduce photographs and illustrations:

Hulton Getty pp. 1, 15.
Mary Evans Picture Library pp. 4–5, 7, 9, 10, 11, 13, 16, 17, 18, 19, 20–21, 22, 24, 26, 27, 28.
The Fotomas Index pp. 3, 12.
Popperfoto pp. 23, 29, 30, 31, 32.

FOR RICHARD HAILL

1

The Battle of Stamford Bridge 1066

Between the seventh and the eleventh centuries Saxon England was a part of the Scandinavian world, torn by internal divisions and open to devastating Viking attacks. Yet in the epic year of 1066 England made a decisive break away from Scandinavia only weeks before William of Normandy's invasion. At Stamford Bridge the Saxons of Harold Godwineson won a total victory over the Norwegian army of Harald Hardrada that, in a sense, brought down the curtain on the Viking Age and by so doing has every right to be considered as decisive a battle as Hastings itself.

The death of Edward the Confessor in 1066 had presented the English with a constitutional crisis. The governing council – the Witan – chose as his successor Harold Godwineson, Earl of Wessex, who had effectively been ruling the kingdom for a decade before the king's death. But Harold had no royal blood in his veins and had found it necessary to marry Edith, sister of the northern earls Edwin and Morcar, to assure the support of the house of Aelfgar for his accession. There were other claimants besides Harold, two of whom were prepared to back their claims by force. On the death of Harthacanute, last Danish king of England, the Danish claim had passed by agreement to King Magnus of Norway. In 1066 his successor, Harald Hardrada, mightiest of Vikings and once commander of the Byzantine Emperor's Varangian Guard, was preparing a Norwegian army to attack England and overthrow the usurper, Harold Godwineson. The second foreign claimant was William the Bastard, Duke of Normandy, who was distantly related to the Confessor and had apparently been promised the throne by him. This rather tenuous claim had been strengthened when Harold Godwineson, shipwrecked in Normandy, had sworn an oath on holy relics to support William's claim when Edward died. But Harold had always claimed that he was tricked into making the oath and denied the Norman charge that he was an oathbreaker. Nevertheless, the Pope declared Harold forsworn and excommunicate, and sent William his banner to show that the expedition to England in 1066 would be a crusade blessed by the Holy Catholic Church.

Harold Godwinson therefore faced a twin threat in the summer of 1066: an attack on the northeast coast by the king of Norway, and an invasion of the south coast by the duke of Normandy. Deciding that the Norman threat was the greater, Harold concentrated his strength in the south, maintaining his fleet between the Isle of Wight and Dover to intercept William's armada, and relying on the earls of Mercia and Northumberland – his brothers-in-law Edwin and Morcar – to face the Norwegians. For much of August the weather was stormy and the wind did not suit William, assembling his forces on the north coast of France. As well as his own feudal troops, William's army was boosted by adventurers from many parts of France and even Italy, who saw the chance of land and booty in England should the duke succeed.

Harald Hardrada, king of Norway, was a formidable warrior, considered the greatest soldier of the age, even though he may not quite have reached the height of seven feet attributed to him by chroniclers. Supported by Tostig, Harold Godwinson's estranged and exiled brother, Hardrada assembled a fleet of 300 ships to launch his attack. Sailing via the Orkneys, Hardrada collected Scottish allies before arriving off the Yorkshire coast, raiding Scarborough and then sailing up the River Ouse before disembarking an army of nearly 10,000 Vikings at Riccall, a few miles from York. Edwin and Morcar called out the northern fyrd (militia) and with their own housecarls (household warriors) they brought the Vikings to battle at Gate Fulford on 20 September. The battle raged all day and ended in a total victory for the invaders. The earls escaped from the bloodbath, but the northern English army had been all but annihilated. Nevertheless, so heavy were the casualties on both sides that the only real winner of the day was William the Bastard, still trapped by the adverse wind conditions in the Norman ports. While Saxon and Viking killed each other his difficult job of conquering England was made easier for him. Neither Edwin nor Morcar took any part in the later fight at Hastings, where even part of their northern army would surely have given Harold victory.

News of the Norwegian invasion was a body blow to Harold Godwineson, still watching the south coast for signs that William of Normandy had put to sea. He faced an agonizing choice whether to stay in the south and leave the north to be ravaged by the Vikings, or to march north to fight Hardrada and leave the south undefended. Ever the man of action, Harold opted to fight the Vikings, knowing that he could hardly expect to maintain the support of the northern earls if he left their lands to the mercy of a pitiless invader such as Hardrada. Assembling his housecarls and those of his brothers Gyrth and Leofwine, and sending messengers north to call out the fyrd of the Midland shires, he began his epic march up the old Roman road of Ermine Street. In one of the greatest forced marches in military history, Harold covered 200 miles or so in six days, surprising Hardrada's troops at Stamford Bridge.

On 24 September, Hardrada's warriors were enjoying a well-earned rest in the sunshine, on the river meadows alongside the Derwent, some eight miles east of York. Many had even removed their armour. Suddenly the glint of sunlight on helmets and shields disturbed their rest. About a mile away a dust cloud indicated the movement of masses of men. The Saxons were upon them. Hardrada ordered his outposts to stand firm and die where they stood, in order to give time for the Norwegians to arm and form up. The Saxons lost no time in charging over the fields towards the bridge across the river, driving the Vikings before them, many of whom drowned in the fast-flowing waters. But now occurred one of the strangest and most heroic incidents of that warlike age. Classical students know of the Roman Horatio who held the bridge single-handed, yet few either in England or in Scandinavia know the equally heroic and undoubtedly true story of the unnamed Viking Berserker who held up the entire English army at Stamford Bridge. For a few minutes on that bloody field everything came to a halt as this huge warrior held one end of the bridge, killing every Saxon who advanced on him. But it could not last. A housecarl found a coracle some way upstream and paddled it under the wooden bridge. He then stabbed the Berserker from below with his spear, through the wooden slats. The bridge was open and Harold's Saxons poured across. By this time the Vikings under Hardrada's personal command had formed up their shield wall and what now took place was a struggle by the housecarls to overcome the Vikings, man for man. Each side fought with battleaxes and swords but it was the housecarls, professional troops of Danish origin, who gained the ascendancy. Several times in this battle the fighting paused while offers were made. King Harold offered his brother Tostig his old earldom if he would abandon the Vikings, but Tostig stayed true to Hardrada and died on the field. The English king famously offered Hardrada six feet of English soil, or seven feet as he was so much larger than ordinary men. We do not know how the Norwegian king eventually met his death but Harold was true to his word and Hardrada was buried on the battlefield.

Eventually, the Saxons prevailed in this tremendous hacking-match with the Vikings. No quarter was asked and none given, so that thousands of Norwegians died upon the battlefield, with hardly fewer Saxons joining them in death. It was the most decisive battle in over two hundred years of Anglo-Viking warfare, extinguishing forever the Scandinavian threat to northern England and, further, virtually ending the 'Viking Age'. In victory Harold proved magnanimous, allowing Hardrada's son Olaf and the young Orkney earls to take the survivors back home. So bloody was the battle that these survivors filled only 24 of the original 300 ships. For the Viking world the battle had proved to be the blackest day in its history. After the battle Harold entered York in triumph, prepared to rest and feast his exhausted army.

2

The Battle of Hastings 1066

William of Normandy's victory at Hastings changed the axis of England's history, freeing the country from its northern links and making it an integral part of the richer Western European world. William turned a wealthy but loosely governed state into a unified and powerful realm, built around feudalism and a hereditary monarchy. William's victory was one of the most significant events of the Middle Ages, and Hastings perhaps the most important battle in England's history.

Even while Harold was freeing northern England from the Viking threat, the wind had changed in the south. William's armada set out from St Valéry on 28 September to make the short crossing of the Channel, landing at Pevensey Bay in Sussex, having avoided the English fleet, which, as luck would have it, was revictualling in the Thames. On landing, William had fallen on his face in the sand – thought by some a bad omen – but he had leapt to his feet saying that thus he had claimed the soil of England. He immediately began ravaging the surrounding country, which he knew to be part of Harold's own earldom, in the hope of making the English king rush precipitately south. William had read his man well. Though Harold was an admirable war-leader, his headstrong nature played into the hands of the more cunning Norman. Harold had everything to gain from moving steadily down to London, bringing what was left of the northern army with him and giving time for the fyrd from distant shires to assemble. In a matter of weeks Harold could have put together an army perhaps three times the size of William's, as well as using his fleet to destroy the Norman ships, on which the duke was dependent for supplies and evacuation in the case of defeat. But Harold was not a man to delay any action and he headed south from York on 1 October, reaching London in six days, leaving Edwin and Morcar's northern army far behind, as well as many of his own housecarls.

Harold stayed in London for just five days, setting out for Sussex with as few as 5,000 men. He collected others as he moved south through the great Andredsweald forest, and when he reached Caldbec Hill another group of fyrdmen were already awaiting him. But it had been another exhausting march over rough tracks, and he had lost many men on the way. Florence of Worcester writes that Harold 'was very sensible that some of the bravest men in England had fallen in the two battles [of Gate Fulford and Stamford Bridge] and that one half of his troops were not yet assembled'. He was certainly outnumbered by William's 6,000–8,000 Normans at this stage, but knew that he would gain reinforcements on the morrow by men drifting in from all quarters. Harold's instinct was for a dawn attack on the Normans, hoping to take them unawares as he had caught Hardrada at Stamford Bridge. But the Norman cavalry pickets reported the English approach to William. In any case, Harold's army was a pale reflection of the one he had taken to York, and he eventually decided that a defence of a position on Senlac Ridge would be the best option.

On 14 October the Normans advanced to Telham Hill and William had his first glimpse of the English army facing him, stretching across Senlac Ridge for about 800–1,000 yards. He could not see Harold but he knew where he would be, standing beneath the great Dragon banner of Wessex and his own personal flag of the Fighting Man – later to be the site of the altar of Battle Abbey. It was a magnificent defensive position, with the English left and centre protected by a steep slope and their right fronted by a marsh, so giving William little option but to attack frontally. The first two ranks of the English army comprised elite housecarls – the best troops in Europe – encased in mail and wielding their fearsome double-handed axes. Behind them, fighting under their thanes (aristocratic commanders), were the serried ranks of the fyrd, some well equipped with helmets, mail and swords, others no more than farm labourers with pitchforks and scythes.

At about 9.30 a.m. William ordered his archers to move into range of the English, and let loose a hail of arrows. However, the housecarls were able to use their shields to give themselves effective protection. As the Norman archers moved even closer to increase the hitting power of their arrows they were met by a hail of English missiles – javelins, throwing axes, arrows and stones – which sent many of them tumbling back down the slope in confusion. The archers had failed to make any impression on the grim line of warriors on the ridge and had, moreover, used up all their arrows. An hour had passed, and William had the extra frustration of seeing the English army reinforced by latecomers who had been marching all night to reach the battlefield.

William now ordered up his heavy infantry, Bretons on the left under Count Alan of Brittany, Normans in the centre, and Flemings on the right under Eustace of Boulogne. In the hand-to-hand fighting that followed both sides suffered heavy casualties, but the housecarls gained the upper hand and sent William's men-at-arms stumbling down the slope in shocked defeat. It was now time for the cavalry to move in to exploit the gaps forced by the infantry – but there were none. As the horses struggled up the steep slopes or through the marshes they lost their momentum, and many of them refused to face the terrible axes of the housecarls, weapons with blades a foot in width, capable of severing a horse's head with one blow. The attack collapsed and William's cavalry fell back in confusion. Now occurred one of the decisive moments of the battle. As the Breton knights retreated, crashing through their own infantry, the chaos they caused threw open the unguarded flank of the Norman centre. Here was a chance for the English to advance with a rush and drive the Normans off the field – but the king had given no order to advance. Whether Harold's brother Gyrth or some thane on the right took the initiative and ordered the fyrd to charge, or whether it was just a spontaneous rush of blood by the untrained shire levies, we will never know. In the event, hundreds of fyrdmen swept aside the housecarls in front of them and charged down the hill in pursuit of the Bretons. At the same moment William fell or was knocked from his horse and the cry went up that the duke was dead. For a few seconds victory lay within Harold's grasp. A charge by the full English line might have so disordered the Normans that they could not recover. But Harold was not sufficiently confident that he had blunted the Norman threat to risk abandoning his strong defensive position. A minute passed. William had leapt to his feet, remounted and removed his helmet, bellowing to his men that he was unhurt. The crisis was over. The Breton cavalry now reformed and massacred their English pursuers, who were trapped in the marshy ground at the bottom of the hill. It is doubtful if more than a handful survived to regain the English lines. It was a disaster for Harold and he knew it. The English line now contracted to take account of the missing fyrdmen.

The three arms of William's force – archers, heavy infantry and cavalry – had now been tried and all had failed in turn. He was left with no option but to engage in the kind of 'toe-to-toe' fighting at which the housecarls were the masters, and so the battle became one of attrition rather than of manoeuvre. The Norman cavalry, quite unsuited to the terrain, struggled through the marshy ground and up the steep slope, only to be turned back with heavy losses time and time again. Then, late in the afternoon, there was an incredible replay of the incident where the fyrdmen charged the Breton knights and were annihilated. So coincidental was this second 'mistake' by the English that many chroniclers have claimed that William's Fleming knights deliberately feigned flight in order to draw out the enemy. This is unlikely, but whatever the reason, the undisciplined English on the left charged down the slope, only to suffer the same fate as their colleagues on the right had met earlier in the day. This second disaster, coming on top of the deaths of Harold's brothers Gyrth and Leofwine, were hammer-blows to the English king, who now must have regretted his decision to give battle with such a depleted army. Yet, drawing in his dauntless housecarls, he presented an unbroken wall of shields and axes to the Normans.

If Harold, on the ridge, was in despair, William was no happier at the bottom of the slope. Only when the English had broken formation had he been able to overcome them. The housecarls had resisted every attack by archer, knight or footsoldier. With only two hours of daylight left, he was afraid that the English would withdraw in the darkness and reform elsewhere, and he knew that his own army could not face a second battle against a reinforced enemy. Victory would have to be won that day – at whatever cost.

Ordering his archers – now with a replenished supply of arrows – to fire in a high arc so that their missiles fell upon the heads of the English, forcing them to lift their shields, William sent in his infantry under this 'creeping barrage'. In the close-quarter fighting on the ridge casualties were again heavy. Inch by inch the Normans gained a foothold, breaking the English line in places and cutting off small groups of men, to be mopped up by the cavalry. In this last stage of the fighting occurred the famous incident of the 'arrow in the eye'. It is impossible to tell from the evidence whether it was Harold or merely a housecarl who was struck in the eye by the arrow. What is certain, however, is that Harold did not die that way. Before the battle a group of Norman knights had sworn to slay the oathbreaker, as they viewed Harold, and though many of them died trying to breach the English line, four eventually broke through the ring of housecarls and hacked Harold down, killing him beneath his banner of the Fighting Man, made for him by his mother, Gytha.

With the death of Harold, English resistance gave way, and the remaining fyrdmen took to their heels and escaped into the forest. The housecarls retained formation and then began to fall back under the attacks of the Norman cavalry. Few leaders were left to organize further resistance – only Esegar the Staller and Leofric, abbot of Bourne, are mentioned. At this moment, in the growing dusk, the Normans suffered a disaster which, had it occurred earlier, would have cost them the battle. Pursuing the housecarls, a large number of riders crashed to their deaths in a ravine – the Malfosse – on the right of the ridge. But it hardly mattered now. While the Norman infantry amused themselves by stripping and hacking the corpses – only Harold's mistress Edith Swansneck could identify his body after the battle – William prepared the next stage of the invasion, the march on London. Harold's body was eventually laid to rest in Waltham Abbey, and William was crowned king in Westminster Abbey on Christmas Day 1066.

3

The Battle of Bannockburn 1314

Robert the Bruce's decisive victory at Bannockburn undid all the work of Edward I, the 'Hammer of the Scots', and secured independence for Scotland. Yet the outcome of the battle should have been very different. In the first place, the English had an overwhelming superiority in numbers and equipment. Poor generalship meant that a powerful English army was so badly misused that it was eventually stranded in a position where it could not manoeuvre, while the potentially 'battle-winning' English archers were hardly used at all and left at the rear of the battlefield.

Edward II's expedition to Scotland in 1314 was aimed at snuffing out Scottish independence once and for all. With him rode many experienced English knights, including Aymer de Valence, who had fought Bruce twice in pitched battles and Sir Giles d'Argentan, who bore the unusual title of 'third best knight of his day'. Edward's total force included about 2,000 knights and 15,000 infantry as well as large numbers of archers.

Edward's army was a large one, greater by far than his son was to employ at Crécy against the French and far superior to the Scottish army of just 6,000 footsoldiers and perhaps 500 horsemen. However, the English infantry was made up of levies of doubtful quality, particularly if compared to Bruce's battle-hardened pikemen, who were generally well trained and were fighting under trusted commanders and for the independence of their homeland. The crucial struggle would be fought between the Scots *schiltrons* (formations of pikemen) and the English knights.

The battle of Bannockburn was fought on terrain quite unsuited to heavy cavalry. Edward's decision to accept battle on the low-lying bogs and ponds of an area next to a tidal estuary was a disastrous one. The problem may have been that he had promised to relieve Stirling by a certain date and thought he could take liberties with an enemy he held in contempt. Yet by accepting combat at Bannockburn, Edward was allowing the Scots to dictate the terms of the encounter. Even the governor of Stirling Castle, Sir Philip Moubray, who had been given a safe conduct to visit the English camp, tried to persuade Edward to wait and see what the Scots did, rather than attack Bruce in the swamps. This was wise advice, but Edward would not listen. His pride was at stake and he declared that he would not turn his back once he had sighted the Scots.

In contrast with the the frenzied atmosphere in the English camp the Scots remained calm. Bruce had divided his army into four 'battles', the first three commanded by his brother, Edward Bruce, the Earl of Moray and Sir James Douglas. The rear 'battle' he commanded himself. Each 'battle' consisted of 1,000–1,500 pikemen, who fought together almost in the fashion of an ancient Greek phalanx. Their formation would be difficult for the English knights to break on their own but they could be easily broken up by a combination of archers and knights, with the horsemen making quick darts into the spaces created by the bowmen. So apprehensive was Bruce of the dangers of the English archers that he had ordered his 500 light horsemen under Sir Robert Keith to attack them as soon as they appeared. He need not have worried, however, for cooperation with lowly archers was the last thing on the minds of the English knights. They were vying with each other for personal honour, a sure sign that the central command of the army was weak.

In addition to his poor deployment of his troops Edward II made an equally bad job of selecting his commanders. Although Humphrey de Bohun, Earl of Hereford, was Constable of England by hereditary right and a bitter rival of the Clare family, Edward decided to appoint Gilbert de Clare, Earl of Gloucester, as Constable for the duration of the battle. Humphrey was an elderly and experienced warrior and regarded Gilbert as just a young upstart who needed to be taught a lesson. By the time the English army approached Stirling these two troublesome nobles had thrown the king's army into chaos.

Although it was getting late in the day Edward's knights were clearly not under his control. Seeing the Scots drawn up in the distance, Hereford and Gloucester charged at them with all their knights, each commander trying to outdo the other. The Scots must have been taken by surprise because Bruce, riding alone in front of his men, was suddenly attacked by Hereford's nephew, Sir Henry de Bohun, who set his lance and charged straight at the Scottish king. It was a famous encounter, but it did not last long. Bruce ducked aside from de Bohun's lance and hit the young knight such a mighty blow with his battleaxe that he split his helmet and his head in half. The elated Scots took this as a good omen and cheered their king as he returned from the combat, holding just the axe handle and lamenting the loss of his favourite weapon.

While Hereford's men were attacking Bruce so unsuccessfully, another English cavalry division, led by Sir Robert Clifford and Henry de Beaumont, had set off northwards to circle round the Scottish army and reach Stirling Castle. To do so they had to pass St. Ninian's kirk. It was here that Moray's 'battle' had been placed to prevent the English trying to outflank the Scots. Seeing the Scottish pikemen advancing, Sir Thomas Grey called on Beaumont to halt. As in so many medieval disasters, when a knight's courage was called into question common sense was tossed to the winds. Beaumont told Grey that he could flee if he wanted, whereupon Sir Thomas and the rest of his knights charged wildly into the mass of pikemen and were quickly speared. In fact, although neither side knew it at the time, the decisive struggle of the entire battle was now taking place. Moray's pikemen were on their own, without the support of their fellows and without the aid of swamp or forest to guard their flanks. Yet the English knights could not break their formation without the support of archers. Eventually, the English knights were driven off and Moray's men were able to rest. But the earl had proved that the English knights alone could not hope to prevail. Unless there were a marked change in English tactics the next day the Scots would certainly win a great victory.

Morale in the English camp was by now very low. In a mood of despondency, Edward made a further mistake, ordering his knights to cross the Bannock Burn and set up camp there. So swampy was the ground that doors and tables had to be taken from a nearby village to take the weight of the horses. The infantry, ignored throughout the campaign, consoled themselves by getting drunk. Few of the English were able to sleep that night, expecting at any moment to be attacked by the Scots. Yet, curiously, the confidence of the Scots was by no means as great as the English may have thought. Having given the English king a 'bloody nose', Bruce was thinking of withdrawing his troops to continue a guerrilla war rather than risk everything on one day's fight. Apparently, it was the news that an English knight – Sir Alexander Seton – had deserted that convinced him English morale was broken and that he should risk battle the next day.

As day dawned the English knights now tried to deploy themselves to face a possible Scottish attack. But they could not find a firm footing anywhere and the improvised walkways of doors and tables could only bear the weight of one horse at a time. Crossing the burn by a number of fords the knights reached some firm ground at last, but on a very narrow front. Here the Scots attacked them. It might be thought that no one in his right mind would use heavy cavalry on so constricted a front where the horses could not even accelerate to a trot, but this was where the English eventually consented to fight. With their horses constantly vulnerable, the English knights had no answer to the massed pikes of the Scots.

It was now that the archers were belatedly brought round to begin firing on the Scottish masses. With no possibility of escape, the Scots pikemen began to fall in large numbers. Had Edward used his bowmen like this from the start and protected them with his knights, the outcome of the battle would have been very different. But now, firing from an exposed position and with no protection, the English archers were swept off the field by Sir Robert Keith's light horsemen. This was virtually the end of Edward's hopes, and Sir Giles d'Argentan with five hundred knights helped to lead the king away from the field and to safety. Having done this Sir Giles rode back into the battle and died on the Scottish pikes.

On seeing the king flee, the English army broke up completely. But as many of the knights were pushed back they began to realize to their horror that there was no real escape. In front were the Scottish pikes, to the rear a treacherous ditch of the Bannock Burn, and on their flanks either swampy ground or the estuary of the River Forth. Panic became widespread and knights, archers and infantry fled in all directions, many drowning in the deep water of the burn. The triumphant Scots pillaged the English camp, in which Edward lost his shield, his seal and all his personal effects. Not since the battle of Hastings had an English king suffered so complete a defeat.

4

The Battle of Crécy
1346

The Hundred Years' War between England and France began as a purely dynastic struggle between princes. However, what began in this way gained in momentum until it became a national struggle by the French people for independence from their English conquerors. What began at Crécy with the triumph of the English longbowmen ended at Formigny in 1453 with the flight of the English in the face of overwhelming French fire from cannons and handguns. Technology had moved on and those who failed to move with it were condemned to succumb to it.

On the death of the French king Charles IV in 1328, the royal line of Capet came to an end and the crown of France passed to Philip of Valois, whose claim was based on the Salic Law of the Franks that property inheritance could not pass through the female line. But Philip was not the only candidate for the crown. Edward III of England believed he had a strong claim to the throne of France through his mother Isabella, daughter of Philip IV, and was prepared to back his claim by force.

The war the English began on 11 November 1337, by capturing the island of Cadsand off the coast of Flanders, took them closer than anyone could have imagined to conquering the whole state of France, at that time the largest and most prosperous state in Europe, with a population of some 20 million and a powerful feudal nobility bred to war, in comparison with England's fewer than 4 million people. Yet comparisons are misleading. England was a far more united state than France, and her soldiers were tough professionals, commanded by a series of brilliant officers with experience from the Scottish wars. And in the longbow the English had a modern, democratic weapon – democratic in that at long range the meanest peasant archer could bring down the greatest noble or the most skilful warrior in all France.

Yet by the time the battle of Crécy was fought in 1346, the effectiveness of the English longbow should have been no secret to the French. English victories at Dupplin Moor in 1332 and Halidon Hill in 1333 against the Scots had been won by a combination of men at arms and bowmen fighting in formation, while at Cadsand in 1337 the English archers had shown their superiority over Flemish crossbowmen. The French themselves had even suffered at the hands of English longbowmen in a number of encounters prior to Crécy, including the naval battle at Sluys in 1340. Yet, incredibly, the French nobility refused to learn from these setbacks and clung to their outdated tactics with limpet-like determination.

Edward III's expedition of 1346 landed near Cherbourg and marched inland, passing unchallenged through the Norman countryside. The town of Caen was captured after a brief siege, and the Constable of France was taken for ransom. The English then moved on towards Rouen, where they learned that King Philip VI was preparing his army and had taken the Oriflamme – the war flag of France – from the Abbey of St Denis in Paris, where it was kept in peacetime. It seemed that at last the French were taking the invasion seriously. Edward now found the bridges across the Seine had been broken down, and so he headed north to rendezvous with his Flemish allies in Picardy. Again he found his way blocked, this time by the River Somme in full flood. And now he found himself closely pursued by a massive French army and was fortunate to find a crossing point near Blanchetaque. He swiftly moved on towards the forest of Crécy, where he took up a defensive position to await a French attack.

Edward III's army was large for the time, consisting of 12,000 men, two-thirds of whom were archers. They held a good position, on a gentle ridge with both flanks protected. On the right flank, nearest to Crécy, was Edward's son, the 16-year-old Edward, Prince of Wales (later known as the Black Prince), along with the Earls of Warwick and Oxford, Count Godfrey of Harcourt, and four 'Garter knights' – Sir Thomas Holland, Sir John Chandos, Lord Stafford and Lord Burghersh. With Prince Edward were 1,000 men-at-arms, 1,000 Welsh footsoldiers and about 3,000 archers. On the left, near the village of Wadicourt, were the Earls of Northampton and Arundel, with the Bishop of Durham and 1,000 dismounted knights, 3,000 archers and some Welsh infantry. The king's reserve 'battle' was situated higher up the ridge, and was made up of 700 dismounted men-at-arms and about 2,000 archers. The chronicler Froissart reports that the English archers adopted a 'harrow' formation for receiving the French charges, and it is clear that Edward III must have been aware of this formation, adopted by the Byzantine general Narses against Totila's Goths at the battle of Taginae in 552.

The French army under King Philip VI was both cosmopolitan and disorganized. As well as the nobility of France, the army included Charles, King of the Romans, the Counts of Namur and Hainault, the Duke of Lorraine and King Jaime II of Mallorca, as well as hundreds of German and Bohemian knights under the blind King John of Bohemia. The French array was one of the largest medieval armies ever assembled, consisting of probably 12,000 mounted men-at-arms, with a vast number of footsoldiers, who were, however, of little value and counted for nothing in French tactics. More significant was the contingent of 6,000 Genoese crossbowmen who preceded the knights into battle, led by their own commanders, Odone Doria and Carlo Grimaldi. The French knights were contemptuous of these mercenaries and ignored their complaints that they were tired after 18 hours of marching and that the continuous rain had soaked their bowstrings.

It was late in the afternoon, and approaching the hour of vespers (6 p.m.) as the disordered French army came into sight of the English. The French king wished to make camp in order to allow the rear of his army to catch up but the undisciplined French knights would not listen to him and pressed on towards their traditional enemies, yelling 'Kill!, Kill!' and causing panic amongst the myriad footsoldiers, who thought battle had already been joined. So poor was the French discipline that, despairing of being able to withdraw his army into camp, Philip decided he had no alternative but to attack.

The Genoese crossbowmen advanced towards the English, followed by the first line of French men-at-arms under the counts of Alençon and Flanders. The first volley from the Genoese crossbows fell short and they began laboriously to reload. They were the most professional troops in the French army and they took their time, unflurried by the apparent stillness of the English lines. Then occurred an epoch-making event in the history of warfare. Never before in three thousand years of human history had a battlefield seen the like of what followed. A storm of arrows burst from the English longbowmen, combined with rocks and debris from the stone-throwing English cannons. It is estimated that inside the next minute 60,000 arrows struck the advancing French army, the most concentrated missile fire from infantry until the nineteenth century.

Not surprisingly, the Genoese were shattered and fled, trying to find shelter from the arrow storm, but unable to break through the masses of French cavalry. In anger at being held up by such mercenaries King Philip called out 'Kill me those scoundrels, for they block our advance and serve no purpose!' There now followed an incredible scene as the king's brother, the Count of Alençon, rode down the retreating Genoese. Soon the area in front of the English was a scene of indescribable confusion. The ground was heaped with bodies, while horsemen tried to ride down their own men and succeeded only in losing all cohesion in the process.

Few of Alençon's first line came to grips with the dismounted English knights, for most were brought down by the arrows, which continued to issue from the English lines in veritable floods. It was like some vast natural disaster. Yet no attempt was made to clear the field before the second French line charged. This resulted in further confusion in which the blind king of Bohemia – fighting chained to one of his knights on either side – was killed.

Throughout the battle the French commanders showed neither tactical understanding nor even common sense. Each band of knights seemed to have the single idea of charging at the enemy head-on, with no thought of manoeuvre or flanking action. The only danger to the English occurred when some of Alençon's men-at-arms, avoiding the archers, managed to break into the division of Prince Edward where they were beaten after a stiff fight. At one stage the young prince was thrown to the ground and was rescued by his standard-bearer, Richard Fitzsimmons. Alarmed at the danger to the prince, Godfrey Harcourt appealed to the king for reinforcements, but Edward issued the famous instruction to 'let the boy win his spurs'. Even so, the king quietly sent the Bishop of Durham with twenty knights to bolster the prince's flank.

The English king was himself engaged in single combat by Sir Eustace de Ribeaumont, and twice knocked to the ground. Eventually, the French knight was overpowered and taken prisoner, and later entertained at dinner. Edward was so impressed by the Frenchman's valour that he gave him a string of pearls, saying, 'Sir Eustace, I give you this chaplet as the best warrior of the day, and I beg you to wear it in the love of me, and seeing you are my prisoner, I give you back your liberty.'

After the French had launched fifteen consecutive charges, the last of which took place in the gathering dusk, they eventually withdrew, having suffered enormous losses, including the kings of Majorca and Bohemia slain, as well as 1,542 lords and knights killed, and thousands of footsoldiers. Philip had been unhorsed twice himself in the fighting, but escaped with some ease as the English, maintaining tight discipline, did not pursue their beaten enemy.

The days of the feudal horsemen were finished, for the longbow and later the handgun, combined with the pike, would give the advantage to the professional footsoldier fighting on the defensive. The French, however, clung to the traditional virtues of knighthood, and the lesson they drew from their defeat at Crécy was the wrong one, that it had been the dismounted English men-at-arms who had triumphed, not the lowly archers. The result was that at Poitiers in 1356 King John II dismounted his knights and advanced these heavily armed warriors towards the English lines on foot. Again the English archers carried out great slaughter, though this time the battle was more of a hand-to-hand mêlée than at Crécy.

Calais was the only direct English gain from the battle of Crécy, yet it was a vital one, becoming a kind of medieval Gibraltar, giving England a foothold on the continent from which to launch invasions, as well as becoming the main port for English wool exports. But more important than that, England had become a significant military power. Her combination of bow and pike was to win her innumerable victories over the French in the next 80 years, allowing her to absorb vast areas of French territory. For 100 years England became the dominant military power in Western Europe.

5

The Battle of Agincourt 1415

By the end of the fourteenth century most of the early gains made by Edward III and the Black Prince in the Hundred Years' War had been lost, but the accession of Henry V to the throne of England in 1413 restored English fortunes. Henry first made an alliance with Duke John 'the Fearless' of Burgundy and then invaded France two years later. His invasion force consisted predominantly of 8,000 archers and 2,000 men-at-arms. After laying siege to and capturing Harfleur, Henry marched his army towards Calais, then an English enclave. It was during his march to Calais that the English encountered a large French army, numbering perhaps 25,000, near the River Somme. At first Henry tried to outmanoeuvre the French but their superiority in mounted troops meant that they always held the advantage and could force the English to stand and fight.

In terrible weather conditions and with most of his men suffering from dysentery (as a result many of the archers marched without hose, much to the amusement of the local French population), Henry found himself with no alternative but to fight the French army, which was under the command of the Dauphin and the Constable of France, Charles d'Albret. The English were heavily outnumbered, with their army reduced by now to just 5,000 archers and 1,500 men-at-arms. As Shakespeare has demonstrated in his famous play *Henry V*, the French knights were overconfident and expected to win easily. This is difficult to credit in view of the numerous occasions on which they had succumbed to English bow and lance tactics. Nevertheless, with superiority of numbers and with a belief that the English were in poor physical shape, the French commanders felt confident of victory.

Early on 25 October, the English army formed up between Tramecourt and Agincourt, with a wood on either flank. In the centre King Henry had only enough men-at-arms to form a single line, with his archers in their famous wedge formation on the wings, protected to the front by pointed stakes that they had cut and hammered into the ground to hamper the French horsemen. About 1,000 yards to the north of them the French had formed up in three lines, mainly of men-at-arms, with the front two lines dismounted, as at Poitiers in 1356, and the rear line mounted. For some four hours the two sides made no attempt to approach one another.

About midday King Henry made a decisive move. He ordered his entire army to advance until they were about three hundred yards from the French. Here he ordered his men to take up their positions again, with the archers hammering in their stakes now within range of the French knights. Surprisingly, the French did not attack the English during their forward movement. Instead, it was the English who took the initiative again. At long range Henry ordered his archers to fire a volley of arrows to gall the French, who responded by charging with cavalry from their flanks. In addition, the dismounted knights led by Charles d'Albret came lumbering forward through the fields of thick mud. It was Crécy all over again. Just as there, the sky was darkened by the English arrows. The French cavalry, unable to face the English arrow storm, turned inwards and charged straight at the men-at-arms. But as they did so they were hit by the archers on both sides. The area in front of the English centre was churned up by agonized horses bucking and tipping their riders in the mud, and charging madly away into the dismounted French knights who were laboriously advancing. Nevertheless, d'Albret's men reached the English lines and drove the English men-at-arms back, but again the archers poured their fire into the heaving French masses. Heavily armoured knights fell or were tipped into the thick mud and trampled underfoot by their fellows. So great was the crush that many of the French knights were unable to wield their weapons at all or even stay on their feet. Choosing their moment, the English archers threw down their bows and, wielding mallets and axes, as well as daggers, charged from behind their stakes and leaped upon the helpless French knights, cracking open their helmets or stabbing them in the face through their visors. Some archers armed themselves with discarded French weapons and brought back to England afterwards swords and lances of the finest craftsmanship. Stories of corpses piled higher than a man may sound far-fetched but in the general crush many died unnoticed and others piled upon them. As one English chronicler related, 'More were dead through press than our men could have slain.' Seeing the terrible scene enacted in front of the English position, the rear line, consisting of mounted French knights, declined to advance, in spite of the urgings of the heroic Duke of Alençon, who rode back and forth between the armies trying to urge the recalcitrant French knights to charge. Despairing of this, he rode into the thick of the English knights until he was struck down close to King Henry. Recognizing the king, he offered to surrender to him but before Henry could take his proffered hand, a furious English soldier killed d'Alençon with an axe-blow. Many French knights had vowed to kill the English king and two English soldiers fought that day wearing the apparel of the king. Both were killed. In addition, Henry's helmet can be seen in Westminster Abbey today dented as it was at Agincourt by a French battle-axe.

The most controversial incident of the battle occurred after the fighting had ceased. By early afternoon the French had either fled or were dead or taken prisoner. But so great was the haul of captives that they virtually outnumbered the entire English army. And in the distance the mounted French knights who had not charged posed a real danger, particularly when the Counts of Merle and Fauquemberghes assembled 600 knights for a new charge. Afraid to risk losing so great a victory, King Henry ordered all prisoners to be executed for fear that they might begin fighting again if the French knights did charge. This was an immensely unpopular decision as many archers were hoping to profit from great ransoms. But the king threatened to hang any man who disobeyed and within minutes thousands of French soldiers had their throats cut. Ironically, the French knights did not charge and so the prisoners wrere killed unnecessarily. Some wounded prisoners were even burned when the houses they were resting in were set alight on the king's orders.

Henry V has been accused of cruel butchery for this massacre but in his position he could scarcely have acted otherwise. French chroniclers were more critical of their own knights whose actions brought about the killing. The eventual deathtoll for the French at Agincourt was a staggering one, probably at least 10,000 died in the fighting and perhaps 2,000 more were killed as prisoners. As at Crécy, the roll call of the dead included the greatest in the land like Constable d'Albret and Alençon, while the live prisoners included Marshal Boucicaut, the Dukes of Orléans and Bourbon, the Counts of Richemont, Eu and Vendôme. English losses were fewer than 500, possibly as low as 100, including the Duke of York, who may have had a heart attack or died of suffocation, and the Earl of Suffolk.

Henry was able to complete his march to Calais after summoning the French herald Mountjoie and informing him that the battle would henceforth be known as 'Agincourt', fought on St Crispin's Day. Won against all the odds, Agincourt is one of the greatest victories of the English and one that set a pattern for a whole tradition of English and British military success.

6

The Siege of Orléans 1429

King Henry V's great victory at Agincourt, in October 1415, paved the way for the conquest of Normandy. The ailing French king Charles VI married his daughter Catherine to the victorious English king and, on the birth of a son, accepted the future Henry VI as heir to both the French and English thrones. But the sudden death of Henry V left his 9-month-old son Henry as king of England under the regency of his uncle the Duke of Gloucester. And when King Charles VI died in turn, the crown of France was there for whoever was strong enough to take it.

The Dauphin immediately proclaimed himself King Charles VII of France, but could not summon up the courage to risk a coronation at Rheims, which was too near English-controlled territory. His weakness summed up the state of France at the time. The Duke of Bedford, with his Burgundian allies, held Paris, while English soldiers like the atrocious Richard Venables and his gang of ruffians roamed freely in lawless bands through much of the country. The military strength of the English, notably the supremacy of their bow and pike tactics, was still too strong for any combination of French knights. At Cravant in 1423 Bedford routed the Dauphin's Armagnac supporters, while the following year at Verneuil he inflicted a great defeat – virtually the equal of Agincourt – on another of the wretched Dauphin's armies. By 1426 Bedford was being drawn into a more widespread campaign aimed at nothing less than the total conquest of the Dauphin's holdings in central and southern France. The future of France as an independent state lay in the balance. It seemed that English military superiority combined with French disunity would achieve the dismemberment of Europe's greatest state.

In October 1428 Thomas de Montacute, Earl of Salisbury, with an English force of 5,000 men, began the siege of the populous city of Orléans, on the River Loire, striking at the very heartland of the Dauphin's strength. If Orléans were to fall to the English, France as an independent kingdom would be virtually extinguished. But two unexpected events were to change the situation completely. On 23 October the Earl of Salisbury, whose very name held terrors for the French, was killed by a stone splinter while overseeing the siege. Even so, French fortunes had further to slip before they recovered. When an English supply column of 300 wagons was approaching the city it was attacked at Rouvray by a large French army. The English commander, Sir John Fastolf, formed up his wagons into a laager (a defensive ring first used by the Hussites) and the escorting English archers destroyed the French in what became known as 'the battle of the Herrings'.

As the English tightened the siege around Orléans, establishing an arc of six stockaded forts to the north of the river Loire, it seemed only a matter of time before the city was forced to surrender. Yet the city had become a symbol of French resistance to English domination, and at this low point the second of the unexpected events occurred: a 17-year-old peasant girl from Domrémy in Lorraine became convinced that it was her destiny to save France from the English. And so began the great French epic of *La Pucelle*, the 'Maid' of Orléans.

Joan claimed that she had heard the voices of the Archangel Michael, St Margaret and St Catherine instructing her to go to the Dauphin's court at Chinon and tell him that it was her task to raise the siege of Orléans and drive the English out of France. Afterwards she was to take the Dauphin to Rheims, where he would be crowned king of France. Having convinced Robert de Baudricourt of her sincerity, she was taken by him the 300 miles to meet the Dauphin at Chinon. Modern views of Joan's probable epilepsy or psychological disturbance are irrelevant. She was what France needed at the time, and her inspiration was enough to convince hard-bitten soldiers like Dunois, Alençon, de Xantrailles, La Hire, Gilles de Rais (later burned for his hideous child-murders and known to history as Bluebeard) and de Richemont (terribly wounded at Agincourt and now with a face like a frog) to follow her as if she were a divine talisman.

Arriving at Orléans, bedecked in a suit of pure white armour, Joan criticized Dunois, the Bastard of Orléans, for his inadequate defence of the city, and set about doing a better job herself. She appealed to the English commanders to raise the siege, sending the following message to Regent Bedford: 'King of England, and you, Duke of Bedford, who call yourself Regent of the Kingdom of France: you, Guillaume de la Poule, Earl of Suffolk: you, John, Sire de Talbot: and you Thomas, Sire d'Escales – who call yourselves lieutenants to the said Duke of Bedford; I call upon you to make submission to the King of Heaven, and to yield into the hands of the Maid, who has been sent hither by God, the King of Heaven, the keys of all the fair cities which you have seized and ravished in France.' At first, Joan sought a peaceful solution. She called on the toughest of the English commanders at Orléans, William Gladsdale, to surrender but received only abuse and threats that if she were caught she would be burned as a witch. Undeterred, she warned Gladsdale that he would die a dreaful death within days. We will never know how Gladsdale received this prediction from the woman he believed to be a witch. All we know is that the morale of the English soldiery sank in the face of Joan's apparently supernatural powers.

The atmosphere in both camps began to change. The previously confident English began to fear defeat while the French soldiers felt hope of victory for the first time. Joan now personally led the assaults against the English positions. In one such action she seized a ladder and placed it against one of the fortifications that the English had built. As she set her foot on the bottom rung she was struck in the chest by a crossbow bolt fired from above. It penetrated six inches into her flesh and she was helped away in apparent agony, pouring blood. Showing incredible courage she refused to lie down in front of her warriors, pulled the bolt out herself and treated the wound with bacon-fat and olive oil, which stopped the bleeding. She could hear the English soldiers exulting at her injury and felt the confidence of her own men ebbing away. She knew that her presence with her men was essential. Raising her own personal standard, she stormed back into the attack, with the French soldiers thronging behind her. She concentrated her efforts on the fortress known as Les Tourelles, commanded by

Gladsdale, which most closely threatened Orléans. Joan's men fought the English hand-to-hand in front of Les Tourelles but even though overwhelmed by superior numbers, Gladsdale refused to surrender and waited for the promised aid from Paris under Sir John Talbot. Yet step by step the English were driven back across a wooden footbridge into their fortress. The French had sailed a fire-ship packed with resin and oil under the bridge and ignited it. The bridge became a blazing inferno and toppled into the Loire, just as Gladsdale was crossing. Half aflame and still shouting defiance, Gladsdale fell into the river cursing the French witch with his dying breath. Half shocked and half elated by the terrible death of her enemy, Joan ordered the body of Gladsdale recovered from the water and given a Christian burial.

The English survivors in Les Tourelles threw down their arms as they saw the death of their commander, calling out that they could see saints and angels fighting with the French. Just two hundred of them were taken alive, the rest died fighting or in the conflagration on the bridge. Joan ordered the church bells in Orléans to ring and throughout the France word spread of her miraculous victory.

The news of the raising of the siege by 'the Maid' and her miracles at Orléans astounded both English and French together. The Duke of Bedford wrote of the 'enchauntements and sorcerie . . . of the Feende, called the Pucelle'. But the English had not abandoned hope of taking Orléans, and the promised reinforcements under Lord John Talbot, known as the 'English Achilles', were hurrying from Paris. Talbot was a doughty professional, much feared by the French, but his contempt for his opponents and his pride in his constant victories made him underestimate the newly inspired French warriors. On 19 July the French army, fresh from its triumph at Orléans, met the English at Patay. Afraid to meet them in an open battle, the French commanders asked Joan's advice. She told them to attack straight away and that they would need their spurs – not to flee, but to pursue the English when they turned tail. Under Joan's inspiration the French defeated the English for the first time in living memory. Moving with such directness that she took her enemy by surprise and before the English had been able to form up their archers in their traditional way, Joan directed her troops to engage in hand-to-hand combat where the English longbows were useless and where superior French numbers were decisive.

Now town after town fell to Joan of Arc's army as it moved north, including the great cathedral cities of Troyes, Chartres and Rheims – where Charles VII was duly crowned on 16 July. Bedford feared that even Paris might fall. And when his army met the French at Montépilloy, Bedford visibly quailed at the sight of Joan's banner among the French flags. Treacherously captured by the Burgundians and presented to the English for trial and execution as a witch, Joan of Arc became a martyr for France, a martyr whose inspiration survived her death. The raising of the siege of Orléans was the decisive moment in the Hundred Years' War. The example of Joan of Arc freed the French people from their obsession with defeat at the hands of the English. Without Joan's inspiration it seems unlikely that Orléans could have resisted for much longer and, having fallen, it would have heralded the collapse of the French monarchy.

7

The Battle of Towton 1461

The unenviable reputation of being the biggest and also the bloodiest battle ever fought in the British Isles is held by the battle of Towton in 1461, in which Edward of York defeated the Lancastrians. It is estimated that a third of all lives lost during the thirty years of the Wars of the Roses, 1455–85, were suffered between dawn and dusk on Palm Sunday 1461 at Towton.

After the defeat of the Yorkists under the Earl of Warwick at St Albans on 17 February, London lay at the mercy of the Lancastrian army; but King Henry VI refused to allow his troops to pillage his capital and eventually he and Queen Margaret withdrew their troops northwards, where they were to be reinforced by troops from the northern counties. Edward of York, fresh from his victory at Mortimer's Cross, occupied London and was proclaimed king by a great crowd of Londoners. Warwick moved into the Midlands and began recruiting new troops from a wide band of counties from the West Midlands to East Anglia. Both sides realized that a decisive battle would soon be fought and both gave unprecedented attention to raising as many men as possible. Some modern statisticians estimate that these remarkable efforts at recruiting meant that one in seven active males in the entire population fought at Towton, with the Lancastrian army at 40,000 only slightly outnumbering the 38,000 Yorkists.

While the king and queen remained in York, command of the Lancastrian army fell to the 24-year-old Duke of Somerset, though there were numerous other peers of the realm present on the red rose side. When news arrived that the Yorkists were advancing from the south, Somerset occupied a ridge between Towton and Saxton, sending Lord Clifford, known as 'the Butcher', forward to dispute the enemy crossing of the River Aire. The result was a

29

full-scale battle at Ferrybridge between advanced Yorkist troops under Lord Fitzwalter and Clifford's Lancastrians. Fitzwalter had found the bridge across the Aire broken down and so he spent much time repairing it. He was surprised in his work by Clifford's men, who drove the Yorkists back across the river, killing Fitzwalter in the process.

News of the disaster reached Edward of York near Pontefract but he refused to panic, sending Lord Fauconberg to cross the river at Castleford and fall on the Lancastrians from the rear. Edward was a giant of a man, six feet four inches as far as we can gather, beloved of the people, particularly women. He it is, of course, whom Shakespeare is describing in the lines, 'Now is the winter of our discontent made glorious summer by this son of York.' Fauconberg was successful, putting the Lancastrians to flight and killing Clifford in the process. The death of the redoubtable Clifford was a great blow to the red rose but it was ample vengeance for Edward whose brother, young Rutland, had been murdered in cold blood by Clifford after the battle of Wakefield, the previous year. To demonstrate his commitment to the Yorkist cause in the forthcoming battle, Warwick slew his horse with his own hand proclaiming, 'Let him fly that will for surely I will tarry with him that will tarry with me.'

The morning of the battle was bitterly cold and windy, with snow blowing across the plateau where the two huge armies moved up to within half a mile of each other. The Yorkist army, marching under the 'Black Bull' banner of Edward and Warwick's 'Bear and Ragged Staff' emblem, was in no hurry to engage, for a substantial element of their army under the Duke of Norfolk had not yet arrived. Still, they could not delay long with such a large force close to them and it was Lord Fauconberg with the Yorkist vanguard who opened the fighting with a clever ruse. The wind was blowing the snow straight into the faces of the Lancastrians. Fauconberg ordered his archers forward to fire a single volley and then retire out of range. With the wind and snow in their favour, the Yorkists naturally outranged their opponents. And when the first volley fell amongst the Lancastrians, their commanders Northumberland and Andrew Trollope ordered their men to return volley after volley. But the contrary wind and the fact that the

Yorkists had retired out of range meant that their arrows fell at least forty yards short and the Lancastrians exhausted their quivers. Fauconberg's archers now stepped forward, replenishing their quivers at their opponents' expense and keeping up a steady fire. Unwilling to stand still under such a storm of arrows, the whole Lancastrian army advanced, and soon a tremendous hand-to-hand struggle began which was to last throughout the day, for possibly as long as ten hours. In this static fighting casualties were enormous and generalship limited. As so often in civil warfare, the bitterness of the fighting was made worse by grudges from previous fights. Quarter was neither asked nor given and the battle line was soon choked with bodies of dead and injured.

The Yorkist left wing was struck by a Lancastrian ambush force which burst upon it from Castle Hill Wood, but in the centre and on the right it was an attritional struggle, with little room for manoeuvre. Somerset's Lancastrian division engaged Edward's Yorkists, while to his left Northumberland engaged Warwick. Sheer weight of numbers began to turn the battle towards the Lancastrians and Edward desperately looked southwards for signs that Norfolk's troops might soon arrive. Step by step the Yorkists were forced back until by midday there was a real danger that they would be defeated. And then came the turning point of the battle. Poor road conditions had slowed Norfolk's march but in the early afternoon Norfolk's banners were sighted advancing from the south. Soon his men began to appear on the right of the Yorkist line. It was literally a blood transfusion. And now the extra men on his right flank allowed Edward to outflank the Lancastrian left and began to roll up their line. Soon Northumberland's soldiers found they were fighting men from front and flank. They began to give ground and look uncertainly to the rear for a means of escape. First a few and then a flood of men began to stumble away from the fight, hindered by their heavy armour and weapons. Now followed the greatest slaughter ever witnessed on British soil. In Bloody Meadow thousands of fleeing Lancastrian soldiers were trapped in the marshy field or drowned in the River Cock. Chroniclers relate how latecomers crossed the river on the piled up corpses of their fellows and the waters ran red as far as the junction with the Wharfe three miles downstream. On the Lancastrian left men fled towards Tadcaster or York, with Yorkist cavalry under Sir John Wenlock harrying them up to the gates of the city itself. It is estimated that 28,000 men died on that day, 20,000 of them Lancastrian. This exceeds the British losses on the first day of the Somme Offensive in 1916.

The Lancastrian leadership was now put to the sword. Edward of York, or Edward IV as we must now call him, had no intention of facing these noblemen again in battle. King Henry and Queen Margaret escaped from York and headed for safety in Scotland, but few of the Lancastrians escaped with them. Entering the city, Edward had the head of his father removed from the Micklegate, where it had been placed by Clifford after the Yorkist disaster at Wakefield a year earlier. Edward replaced it with the head of the newly executed Lancastrian peer, Thomas Courtney, Earl of Devon. Afterwards, leaving the Earl of Warwick and Richard of Gloucester to control the north, Edward headed back to London with most of his nobles to prepare for his coronation. The decisive battle of the Wars of the Roses had been fought and won.

8

The Battle of Bosworth Field 1485

The defeat and death of Yorkist King Richard III in 1485, at the battle of Bosworth Field, marked not just the final act in the story of the Plantagenet family, which had occupied the English throne since the accession of Henry II in the twelfth century, but in a sense it also marked the end of the Middle Ages in England. With the coming to power of the Tudors, England moved towards a more united kingdom in which the nobility found service with the crown rather than as independent warlords, making and breaking kings and constantly feuding amongst themselves. And if Bosworth Field was no dramatic battle – there was no Shakespearian Richard 'Crouchback' offering his kingdom for a horse – yet few military encounters in English history were so pregnant with consequences.

Henry Tudor's accession to the throne of England in 1485 as Henry VII was the final act in what have become known as the 'Wars of the Roses'. He had no strong claim to be king, but so many better placed candidates had died in the previous thirty years of internecine strife that by 1485 he, through his mother Margaret Beaufort, was the head of the Lancastrian faction. Henry had spent the previous fourteen years in exile in Brittany with his uncle Jasper Tudor, while the Yorkists ruled in England. But he did not abandon hope and kept in touch with other exiled Lancastrian lords, waiting for his chance to return to England.

In April 1483 King Edward IV died, leaving the crown to his 12-year-old son Edward, and the government of the country to his brother Richard of Gloucester, as protector. Richard had been loyal to his brother while he lived, but now he had no intention of allowing the new king's Woodville relatives to keep him from power. In

May, with the support of the Duke of Buckingham, Richard placed the young king and Richard of York, his brother, in the Tower of London 'for their comfort'. Then, proclaiming his brother's marriage to Elizabeth Woodville invalid, Richard declared Edward's two young sons bastards. After they had been secretly murdered (on whose orders is still a matter of fierce debate) Richard had himself declared king on 6 July 1483. But taking the throne was easier than keeping it. Both at home and abroad Richard III faced many enemies. In France the Lancastrian lords had gathered around Henry Tudor as their champion, while in England the king had reason to fear that powerful families, such as the Stanleys in the northwest and the Percys in Northumberland, would prove false in a crisis. As news of Richard's unpopularity reached France, Henry Tudor's advisers convinced him that his chance had come.

Henry Tudor's fleet left Harfleur on 1 August, carrying with it a force of 2,000 French mercenaries under the command of Philibert de Chaundé. With Henry were a number of English lords who had shared his exile, including his uncle Jasper Tudor, John de la Vere, Earl of Oxford, and the Bishop of Ely. Six days later, 'with a soft southern wind', a landing was made at Milford Haven, in Pembrokeshire, part of Jasper Tudor's earldom, where Henry had spent his own boyhood and was sure of support.

The news that reached King Richard of his rival's progress must have been galling. As the rebels marched through Wales it was clear that neither Sir Walter Herbert in the south nor Sir William Stanley in the north would try to bar Henry Tudor's way. Richard was so unsure of his friends that he felt obliged to tie them to him. When Lord Stanley asked permission to return to his estates in Lancashire on the grounds of ill health, Richard agreed but only on condition that his son, Lord Strange, should remain as a hostage.

Meanwhile, Henry Tudor had reached Shrewsbury – where he was joined by Sir Gilbert Talbot with 500 men – and next turned south, passing through Staffordshire. Ominously for the king, both Lord Stanley and his brother William had already met with the rebels at Atherstone; Richard now knew that they could not be relied on for support in the coming struggle. Only the fact that the king held Lord Stanley's son might persuade them at least to remain neutral. From his headquarters at Nottingham castle Richard had been following the progress of the invaders, but once they moved into Leicestershire he decided that the time had come to strike in case they slipped by him and made a dash for London. On 19 August he set off at the head of the royal army for Leicester. He still had a substantial advantage of numbers, and his force of about 8,000 men marched in three separate 'battles': in the van were 1,200 archers and 200 knights led by John Howard, Duke of Norfolk; the main battle of 2,000 pikemen and 1,000 men armed with halberds and bills was in his own charge; while the rear battle, led by Henry Percy, Earl of Northumberland, consisted of 2,000 billmen, with 1,500 horsemen, who also rode along the flanks of the march. It was a strong, professional force under proven commanders – both Richard and Norfolk had gained battle experience under Edward IV – but its loyalty was doubtful.

The royal army met the invaders near the village of Sutton Cheney, and the foremost of Norfolk's troops took up position on Ambion Hill. The Stanley brothers, with 5,000 of their personal retainers, were also in the vicinity: Sir William to the north of the royal army and Lord Stanley to the south. They were either maintaining a neutral position until they saw which side was likely to emerge victorious, or else merely waiting for the right moment to attack the king. On the morning of 22 August the royal army took up its battle positions and the king sent his last message to Lord Stanley, telling him that unless he joined the royal army his son would be executed. It is said that Stanley boldly replied that he had other sons and would not come. As it happened Lord Strange was not killed – surprisingly, in view of Richard's subsequent reputation.

The Earl of Oxford led the vanguard of the rebel army, which, before it could reach Norfolk's men on Ambion Hill, had to cross the swampy ground at the foot of the ridge. This difficult terrain threw Oxford's men into confusion, and for a while the advantage lay entirely with the king. Had he chosen to charge down the hill onto Oxford's disordered ranks, he would probably have routed them and won the battle before it had really started, but he missed the opportunity. Perhaps Richard was overconfident and held his opponents in contempt, or else he felt that he could not trust his own troops. If the latter was true, he had good reason to be suspicious for, as the chroniclers tell us, there were many of the royal army 'who rather coveted the king dead than alive, and therefore fought faintly'. The moment passed and Oxford soon restored order to his troops. Next he brought up some artillery and opened fire on the massed ranks on the hill above him. The cannon caused little damage but its effects were psychological. The noise and unusual threat posed by the explosions depressed Norfolk's men, whose morale was already low.

Oxford now gathered his men around his personal standard – a star with streams – ordering that no man should break ranks. As the rebels marched up the hill in a bristling phalanx of pike and billmen the serious fighting began, a hand-to-hand struggle that lasted for two hours. It was a desperate struggle between men fighting less for a cause than to save their own lives. Tactics were simple: as gaps appeared in the front lines more men were fed into the mêlée from the main bodies behind; in such fighting, weight of numbers would eventually tell. But morale was as vital as numbers, and when the Duke of Norfolk was killed, some say by Oxford himself, the royal army began to waver. A messenger was seen riding to Sir William Stanley with the news of Norfolk's death and the capture of his son, the Earl of Surrey. It was what the Stanleys had been waiting to hear: Richard III was doomed.

Meanwhile, from his position in the centre of his troops, Richard could see that the day was turning against him. His rearguard, led by Northumberland, was refusing to move up to his support. It was at this moment that the most dramatic action of the battle occurred. Some chronicles report that Richard undertook a royal 'death-ride'. Since the start of the fight Richard had been calling on keen-sighted men to pick out the exact position of Henry Tudor in the rebel army. Convinced that only the death of his rival on the field could change his fortunes, Richard mounted his white charger and, battleaxe in hand and with his personal bodyguard of 80 knights around him, he rode down the slopes of Ambion Hill, heading straight for Henry Tudor. Hacking his way through the ranks of Welsh footsoldiers, Richard struck down first Sir John Cheyney, a man far taller and stronger than himself, and then Sir William Brandon, Henry's personal standard-bearer. But at this moment, Sir William Stanley's men, who had been merely watching the struggle so far, attacked the right flank of the royal army. In the confused fighting around Henry Tudor's standard, Richard III was pulled from his horse and impaled on a mass of Welsh pikes before he could find his enemy.

All around the royal army was breaking up under the combined weight of Henry's French and Welsh troops to their front and the retainers of the Stanley brothers now worrying their flanks. According to the chronicles, Richard's crown was found on a thorn bush and taken by Lord Stanley to crown Henry Tudor on the battlefield. This was a fitting climax to a battle that had turned entirely on the treachery and dishonour of the Stanleys. What courage had been shown came from the king himself, who died fighting – only the second English king to die in battle at the head of his men.

Casualties were light, for there was no point in fighting once the king was dead. The royal army lost perhaps 1,000 men to the rebels' 200, though as was usual in battles of this period, casualties were proportionately higher among the nobles. In death Richard was exposed to a shame that mirrored the hatred felt for him by his many enemies: his naked body was slung across the back of a horse and exposed publicly in Leicester for two days before being buried at Greyfriars church.

9

The Battle of Flodden 1513

James IV of Scotland was unfortunate to be born as the age of chivalry was coming to an end and being overtaken by an age which drew its inspiration from the teachings of Machiavelli. As Cervantes demonstrated in his novel *Don Quixote*, those who failed to adapt were condemned to extinction. In England the ruthless Henry Tudor (Henry VII) adapted successfully and bequeathed a stronger nation-state to his posterity. In Scotland, on the other hand, the well-loved King James died, full of honour, on the battlefield of Flodden, in the front ranks of his men. As a result, Scotland was condemned to a hundred years of foreign domination, first French and then English, and all this just two hundred years after Robert the Bruce had secured independence for Scotland at Bannockburn.

The creation of a Holy League in 1511 brought Henry VIII of England into alliance with the Holy Roman Emperor Maximilian. Their target was to combat the growing power of France and they created a tight ring of allies around the French, who in turn looked to Scotland to keep the English occupied at home. The French queen, Anne of Brittany, appealed to the chivalric character of King James, calling on him as her true knight to advance into England and do battle in her name. So when in 1513 Henry VIII of England invaded France with 25,000 men, James prepared to honour his promise to the French.

Claiming that once Henry VIII had left for France with his army, 'only millers and mass priests' remained in England, James assembled his army near Edinburgh. It was probably the largest army ever assembled in Scotland and its size alone indicates that James expected to face a tougher challenge than merely millers and priests. Estimates range between 30,000 and 40,000 men preparing to invade England, and with these marched a small

French contingent under the Count d'Aussi, who had already been instructing the Scots in modern tactics and the use of the long pike, a dominant weapon in the hands of the Swiss or the German *Landsknechts*. As well as 6,000 pikemen, the Scots also possessed 1,000 handgunners and James's pride and joy, his train of heavy artillery, made for him in Scotland by Scotland's master gunner, Robert Borthwick.

Hearing of Scottish preparations, Henry VIII wrote from France to the Earl of Surrey, his Lord Lieutenant of the North, warning him 'forget not the old prankes of the Scottes which is ever to invade England when the King is out'. Surrey assembled his army at Newcastle. It was something of a family affair, with his son Thomas, the Lord Admiral, joining him with 1,000 marines from the fleet, and his brother Edmund also among the commanders. Surrey brought with him to the rallying point the banner of St Cuthbert which had been carried at earlier battles with the Scots, such as Neville's Cross and the Standard, as long ago as 1138. Unlike the armies that England had been sending to France for the previous two hundred years it was not a professional force, but resembled more a feudal force of retainers attending on their lords. Numbering perhaps 26,000 men, with the majority archers or billmen but with small contingents of cavalry or gunners, it was facing a larger and better equipped Scottish army and would rely heavily on the abilities of its generals. Surrey himself was seventy years old and was no longer fit enough to ride to the field. Instead he was carried about by coach. Yet, however feeble his body, there was nothing wrong with his mind, for he was an astute general, as events were to show.

Surrey prepared to play Machiavelli against King James's Don Quixote, recognizing the need to use every weapon at his disposal against the Scots, even psychological ones. The Scots' king was well known for his love of honour and Surrey therefore challenged him to come forth and give battle like a gentleman, hoping to persuade him to give up his advantage of the high ground, which the Scots had occupied at Flodden Hill. It was a cunning ruse. Surrey sent James a challenge 'to gyve the sayde Kinge batayle by Frydaye next at the furthest'. But the challenge only partially worked. Clearly, however keen James was to give battle, his French advisers preferred not to lose the advantage of the high ground and stayed on Flodden Hill. Surrey now resorted to a well-chosen insult addressed to King James: 'it hath pleased you to chaunge your said promyse and putte yourself into a grounde more like a fortresse or a campe.' The king was irked, responding: 'it beseemed not an erle, after the manner to handle a Kynge.'

Meanwhile, the Scottish army spanned the complete mile or so of Flodden Hill and was divided into five divisions, one of which was held in reserve under the Earl of Bothwell. On the left were the Borderers, commanded by Lord Home, along with the Earl of Huntley's Highlanders; next came the troops of the Earls of Errol, Crawford and Montrose; in the centre was the largest division, commanded by King James himself, while on the extreme right were the Highlanders of Argyll and Lennox. It was an imposing force in an apparently impregnable position.

Surrey realized that it was impossible to defeat the Scottish army on Flodden Hill so he resolved to make them abandon it, either through fear that he intended to bypass them and invade Scotland himself, or by presenting the Scots with an unmissable chance to defeat him as he manoeuvred his forces below them. Surrey therefore showed great boldness in ordering his army to march northwards, apparently ignoring the Scots – in heavy rain it was a dismal march for his men through bogs and swampy heathland, and they were forced to cross the River Till, by bridge and by ford – leaving himself in danger of being attacked on the move. The Lord Admiral's division led the advance, with Surrey's division as much as a mile behind. It was a calculated risk, but Surrey's army had not eaten for a day or more and he was desperate to bring on the battle before he would have to resort to revictualling. At first the Scots disappointed him. Instead of charging down to attack him they simply moved north themselves by keeping to the high ground and formed up on Branxton Hill.

With the two armies just 600 yards apart it was time for the artillery to open fire. In the poor visibility the Scottish gunners fired well over the English troops, while the inferior English guns proved surprisingly effective, firing point-blank into the massed troops on the Scots' left. The noise was tremendous and men on both sides fled in fear. Nevertheless, the artillery fire soon achieved everything Surrey had failed to achieve by cunning. The battle began with the usual display of indiscipline by the Scots, with the borderers, impatient at being bombarded by the English cannon, charging down from their ridge and with them carrying the Highlanders of Huntley's command. They smashed straight into Edmund Howard's division, unhorsing Howard himself and sending a Cheshire contingent fleeing from the field. Their momentum carried them deep into the English ranks but there the fighting became more static. At that moment, Surrey rescued the situation by sending Lord Dacre's horsemen to blunt the Scottish progress. Significantly, the Scottish left wing began looting the dead and rustling the English horses that were corralled nearby. As a result, these borderers played little part in the rest of the fight. Their commander, Home, was later executed for alleged treachery. It was said that he and Dacre, as neighbours, had reached an agreement not to fight any further.

The precipitous charge of the left wing persuaded King James to order the rest of his army to charge down from Branxton Hill. It may have seemed that his left wing had already broken the English right and that the battle was almost won. If he thought this he was sorely mistaken. The two central divisions, under Bothwell and the king himself, came slithering down the slippery slopes, following the blue and white banner of St Andrew. Here the ground actually rose towards the English centre and the Scots found themselves at a considerable disadvantage, particularly for heavily armoured soldiers carrying pikes at least eighteen feet in length, advancing in heavy rain and across slippery ground. So treacherous were conditions it is said many men removed their boots to get a better grip. As the Scots advanced, the fire of the English cannon as well as the archers inflicted casualties, causing a pile-up of bodies in front of the advancing phalanxes. For two hours the Scots struggled to come to grips with the English, all the time losing more and more men to missile fire. Many Scots, unhappy with their pikes, threw them aside and resorted to their swords, making them easy targets for the English billmen. It was not until darkness fell that the Scots in the centre gave up the struggle and began drifting away from the fight, heading for home.

Essentially, the battle was won and lost even before the two sides came to grips. The French attempts to modernize Scottish tactics and introduce the long pike on the Swiss fashion was a complete failure. The Scots lacked the necessary discipline and found the weapon impossibly cumbersome. At Flodden, the English billmen and halberdiers simply hacked the unwieldy pikes to pieces and then clove their owners like sides of meat. King James of Scotland died under a welter of heavy blows to his head just as Charles the Bold of Burgundy, a similarly rash commander, had died at Nancy in 1477, both so disfigured that they could hardly be identified. It took Lord Dacre, who knew King James well, hours of searching amongst the bloody corpses to find the body of the Scottish king. Surrey later had the body embalmed and returned to Scotland. King James's bloody surcoat was especially valued and was sent to King Henry in France, who proudly showed it to the Emperor Maximilian.

Meanwhile, the Highlanders on the right of the Scottish army had paid a heavy price for their lack of armour, being shot down in their hundreds by Lord Stanley's archers. Once he had put the Highlanders to flight, Stanley struck the Scottish centre from the flank. Already, the centre of the Scottish army was leaderless as most of their commanders had followed the king's example and fought in the front ranks, being among the first to be killed.

The losses suffered by the Scots were enormous. In the long history of Anglo-Scottish warfare the battle of Flodden stands far above any other encounter as a disaster for Scotland. Probably 10,000 Scots died that day as well as a whole generation of the nobility. Ten earls were killed on the field, as well as thirteen barons and ninety heads of clans. English losses, heaviest in Edmund Howard's division, were relatively light, though figures of just 400 given by chroniclers are far too low.

Henry VIII rewarded the Howard family for its loyalty. Old Surrey, who had fought for King Richard III at Bosworth Field and been captured, regained the family dukedom of Norfolk in 1514, while his brother Edmund was knighted and his son Thomas gained the title of Lord Surrey. Old Surrey had preserved northern England from the Scots and won a victory without parallel in Anglo-Scottish history. Bannockburn was more than avenged.

10

The Battle of Marston Moor 1644

The term 'Cavalier' has entered the English language as both a description of the supporters of King Charles I during the English Civil War and as an adjective which described the way so many of these men thought about war in general. Thus 'cavalier' has come to mean 'rash, incautious, wild', the very qualities which inspired Prince Rupert of the Rhine, nephew of the King and commander of his cavalry. Usually Rupert demonstrated them in battle, where his 'wild' and 'desperate' charges carried all before him and won victories over his more cautious Parliamentary opponents. However, in seeking battle at Marston Moor, in 1644, his 'rashness' and 'over-confidence' allowed his enemies to win a victory so decisive that the Royal cause never recovered. Defeat cost Charles I his northern capital and most of his northern army.

During June 1644 three Parliamentary armies besieged the city of York, then held by the king's northern commander, the Earl of Newcastle. Charles had sent Prince Rupert northwards to save the city, intending that if this could be done without a battle, then Rupert should avoid the risk of fighting at a numerical disadvantage.

On the morning of 1 July Rupert completely outmanoeuvred the enemy and reached York, linking up with Newcastle's army in the city. King Charles would have been the first to tell Rupert that he had already done enough; there was no need to risk a battle that had already been won by manoeuvre. But Rupert was feeling over-confident and, rather than resting his troops and attempting to weld a unified command with Newcastle, he decided to bring on an immediate battle.

The Royalist commanders in York – survivors of a long, hard siege and perhaps less 'cavalier' than the prince – were alarmed by Rupert's plan and tried to dissuade him. The Earl of Newcastle was expecting at any time 5,000 reinforcements from the north under Colonel Clavering. But Rupert refused to wait for them, insisting that he had a 'command from the King to fight the Scottish army whereso'er he met them'.

Meanwhile, the allied Parliamentary and Scots leaders had just heard disastrous news from the south. King Charles had won a victory at Cropredy Bridge in Oxfordshire and they therefore began to withdraw towards Tadcaster. But Rupert wanted to force a battle on Marston Moor, so that the Parliamentarians hastily recalled their infantry, which was stretched out in straggling columns on the road south, expecting at any moment to be attacked by a torrent of Rupert's cavalry.

Rupert had his own troops in position by early morning on 2 July, but he had agreed to wait for the rest of the army – mainly the York garrison – to march out from the city. Gazing in frustration across the broad moor, Rupert's officers could see that the enemy was in complete confusion, assembling amid standing corn and hedges and with little room to manoeuvre on ground turned marshy by the summer rain. But as the morning dragged on, there was still no sign of the city garrison arriving on the field. When at last Newcastle and his Lifeguards arrived it was approaching midday. Rupert was furious but struggled to keep his temper: 'My Lord, I wish you had come sooner with your forces.'

Across the moor the Parliamentarians were in a shambles as troops took up position more or less as they arrived, with the Scottish infantry, which had headed the march to Tadcaster, being the last to return. But by about 2 or 3 p.m. they had completed their preparations, and by the time Eythin arrived at about 4 o'clock, with 3,000 foot and not the 4,000 Newcastle had promised, it was to find the enemy confidently singing psalms. Rupert now faced an enemy army that outnumbered him by 27,000 to 17,000. The second greatest battle ever fought on English soil was about to take place.

On the right of the Parliamentary army were the 3,000 cavalry of Lord Fairfax's Northern Army, commanded by his elegant son, Sir Thomas Fairfax. In the centre was the mass of footsoldiers, some 16,000–18,000 strong, containing a majority of Scots. Most of the footsoldiers were pikemen, but there was also a proportion of musketeers. The pikemen were gathered together in regiments of 1,000 men and armed with 16- to 18-foot pikes. On the left of the Parliamentary army was the elite cavalry of the Eastern Association (troops drawn from East Anglia), commanded by Oliver Cromwell and numbering over 5,000 men.

As overall commander of the Royal army, Rupert did not lead the cavalry as was his custom. Instead he took a calculated risk in choosing the brave but impetuous Byron to command the right wing. Byron's unreliability was well known: his headstrong charge at Edgehill in 1642, in support of Rupert, had done much to deprive the king of a complete victory on that day. Yet so important was Byron's responsibility that the prince gave him explicit instructions on how to face the charge of Cromwell's cavalry. It was common practice at that time to intermingle musketeers with cavalry on the pattern of tactics by King Gustavus Adolphus of Sweden, and Byron's front line was made up of 1,100 horse, with 500 musketeers in platoons of 50 placed between the regiments of cavalry. As a flank guard for Byron, Colonel Tuke's regiment of 200 horse was placed on his right. Behind the front line was a second line of 1,300 horse, under Lord Molyneux, containing Prince Rupert's own regiment. However, Rupert went further than this and improvised a 'forlorn hope' of some 1,500 musketeers under Colonel Thomas Napier along the ditch that crossed the battlefield parallel with the Marston road. Under no circumstances, Byron was told, should he charge out against Cromwell. He was to wait until the Roundheads had been disordered by the terrain and the fire of the musketeers before joining battle.

Rupert had placed both his and Newcastle's infantry – to the number of about 10,000 men – in the centre, under the command of Lord Eythin. The quality of these troops varied greatly, from the recently recruited Lancashire men, who threw down their arms in many cases at the first clash, to the veteran 'whitecoats' – Newcastle's 'lambs' – who were the best infantry on the field, and fought to the death.

On the left Rupert gave the command to the general of the Northern Horse, George Goring, a drunkard away from the battlefield but a brave and shrewd general, and to his stalwart lieutenant-general, Sir Charles Lucas. Here the Royalists enjoyed a considerable advantage in terrain, which they were to put to good use. Rupert kept personal control of a reserve of 700 horse.

As afternoon passed into evening, battle seemed less and less likely and the Prince declared that he would not attack until the next morning. When Newcastle asked if he was certain that the enemy would not attack him, Rupert arrogantly dismissed the possibility that a dullard like the Scotsman Lord Leven – the Parliamentary commander-in-chief – could take him by surprise. Rupert meanwhile ordered food to be brought from York for the whole army, while he and his troopers dismounted and began their meal.

Although illiterate and of humble stock, Alexander Leslie, 1st Earl of Leven, had more professional experience than Rupert. Perhaps he had none of the prince's flair, but he had learned his craft in the Swedish service under the best European captains, and he knew when his enemy had dropped his guard. Just as a storm of rain began, discomforting Rupert's musketeers, Leven ordered his cannons to fire, and signalled the entire Parliamentary army to advance.

On the left Cromwell had been bombarding Byron's position for some while, and the Royalist cavalry was eager to charge and must have pressed Byron to take some retaliatory action. Byron needed little persuasion to disobey his orders and, at the sight of Cromwell's cavalry charging down towards him, he set out to meet them, scattering his own musketeers, whom Rupert had placed with such care. Byron's 'cavalier' disregard for his orders was to hand victory to the Parliamentary cause. When Cromwell's troopers smashed into Byron's line in the marshy area and broke it, sending its scattered remnants fleeing from the field, there were no musketeers left to stop the Ironsides. With Byron beaten, the second line led by Viscount Molyneux now made a determined resistance, standing like an 'iron wall' against the Roundheads. Cromwell was himself wounded at this stage and temporarily forced to leave the field for treatment. Molyneux and his brother, both 'blood-thirsty Papists', fought with particular bitterness against David Leslie's Presbyterian Scots until overwhelmed by sheer weight of numbers.

When the fighting began, Rupert was 'set upon the earth at meat a pretty distance from his troops, and many of his horsemen were dismounted'. In a matter of minutes, he gathered his Lifeguards and rode towards the right wing in time to see Byron's troops beaten and his own regiment fleeing. It was at this moment that the prince's white pet poodle 'Boy' was shot dead. 'Boy' always accompanied Rupert to every battle and the Parliamentarians believed that he was no dog but the prince's familiar spirit.

On the other side of the field, however, things went differently. Sir Thomas Fairfax's cavalry faced serious man-made obstacles. In order to reach the moorland Fairfax was forced to channel his cavalry, which contained many raw recruits, through a narrow lane, which the Royalists had lined with musketeers. As he tried to do this, Goring led a counter-charge that drove the Parliamentary cavalry off the field. Fairfax found himself alone, slashed through the cheek and without a command. But instead of fleeing with his men he remained to play a prominent part in the later stages of the fighting. Removing the 'signal out of my hat' – a white scarf for identification – 'I passed through for one of their own commanders' and rode unnoticed across the battlefield before joining up with Cromwell on the other side of the moor.

Goring's Northern Horse had meanwhile reached the ridge from which Fairfax had set off. Here he 'possessed many of their ordnance and, if his men had been kept close together as did Cromwell's, and not dispersed themselves in pursuit, in all probability it had come to a drawn battle at worst . . . but Goring's men were much scattered . . . before they could know of the defeat of the Prince's right wing'. Many of Goring's men were plundering enemy baggage tents and it is doubtful if he had even 1,000 men under control as night drew on. Sir Charles Lucas, leading the second line of Goring's wing, found the flank of the Parliamentary infantry completely open and savaged the unguarded Scottish pikemen, spreading such panic through the right of the allied army that all three of its commanders fled from the field: Leven to Leeds, Lord Fairfax to his house at Nun Appleton, where he went to bed, and the Earl of Manchester, who was eventually prevailed upon to return. Rumours of defeat spread down the road with them, and in

47

the Royalist town of Newark the church bells signalled a great victory for the king. But as a Scottish army chaplain commented, 'God would not have a general in the army; He himself was general.'

And if God needed a tool that day, he chose Oliver Cromwell. As Cromwell wrote, 'God made them as stubble to our swords.' Having scattered the Royalist right wing, he led his cavalry round the back of the Royalist infantry so that he now took up the position originally occupied by Goring's Northern Horse. Darkness was closing in and, on a battlefield thick with the smoke of thousands of muskets, it must have been almost impossible to see what was going on. But Cromwell had chosen the right moment to strike the decisive blow. With nearly 4,000 cavalry still in hand, he was looking up the slope at Goring's victorious – but disordered – Northern Horse, probably no more than a quarter of his own strength.

This time Goring would have to fight on the disadvantageous ground that had proved too much for Fairfax earlier in the fight, and with greatly inferior numbers. Nevertheless, Goring flung his troopers down the slope towards the enemy, only to be shattered by the impact. As the Northern Horse fled from the field, Cromwell reined in as many squadrons as he could. The battle might be won; but there was still God's work to be done or if not God's, at least the Angel of Death's.

In the centre of the moor the heavily outnumbered Yorkshire infantry had refused quarter and, with no cavalry left to support them, prepared to fight to the death. As one observer wrote, 'Our foot play'd the man, but the horses jades.' To save the useless slaughter of brave men, Sir Thomas Fairfax rode into the fray, beating up the weapons of his own men and shouting, 'Spare your countrymen', but Newcastle's own whitecoat regiment fought on until overrun by Parliamentary cavalry. Their coats of undyed woollen cloth led their enemies to gloat that they had 'brought their winding-sheets about them into the field'. Just three of their number survived the battle.

With the Parliamentary leaders having fled, it was left to Oliver Cromwell to complete the victory. York, so recently relieved, now fell to Parliamentary forces along with most of the north of England. The Earl of Newcastle, the king's main supporter in the north, fled to the continent, along with Lord Eythin and many prominent Royalists. Thus it was left to Prince Rupert to rally the remnants of the king's army. When he next met his monarch it was not as the liberator of York but as the man who had lost the war 'while eating his supper'. Rumours that Rupert had escaped from Marston Moor by hiding in a bean field were probably untrue but certainly the battle has a claim to uniqueness, based on the fact that by the time that it ended all six commanders – Leven, Lord Fairfax and Manchester on the Parliamentary side and Rupert, Eythin and Newcastle on the King's – had fled the field, leaving younger officers of the next generation like Oliver Cromwell and Sir Thomas Fairfax to gather the spoils.

11

The Battle of Blenheim 1704

A century before Napoleon, Britain faced an equally dangerous European foe in the France of Louis XIV, determined to secure hegemony in Europe. For William Pitt the Younger one must read King William III and for the Duke of Wellington John Churchill, the first Duke of Marlborough. The victories Marlborough achieved on the continent were the greatest by a British commander before Wellington and restored the balance of power in Europe. The final stage in this great struggle was known as the War of the Spanish Succession, which broke out in 1702 and coincided with the death of William III and the accession of his daughter, Anne. Louis XIV of France refused to recognize her, accepting instead the Jacobite candidate, James Stuart – the Old Pretender – as the rightful king of England. England's allies – the United Provinces in the Netherlands and the Austrian Habsburgs – were both ailing by this time, and with France's ally the Elector of Bavaria coveting the Imperial throne at the expense of the Habsburgs, the future for the English cause in Europe seemed bleak indeed. Yet in one of the greatest campaigns in military history, Marlborough marched an army 300 miles from the English Channel to southwest Germany and inflicted a defeat at Blenheim on the Franco-Bavarian forces threatening Vienna, shifting the entire balance of power in Europe in favour of England and away from France for the next hundred years.

In May 1704, Marlborough began his famous march along the eastern bank of the Rhine, outmanoeuvring his French opponents, who entirely failed to detect his purpose. It was a masterpiece of logistics, marching an army through enemy territory and in the face of vastly superior forces. Marlborough used bluff to confuse both enemies and allies alike, finding it safer that way. Along roads turned into muddy rivers by unseasonal weather Marlborough maintained a steady ten miles a day with a full rest day every fifth and with carefully prepared campsites ready for the toiling troops at day's end. Fresh shoes, clothes and provisions were constantly available and when he arrived at the Danube and linked up with his ally, Prince Eugène of Savoy, his army was still in prime condition. As one participant commented, 'Surely never was such a march carried out with more regularity and with less fatigue to man and horse.' Only 900 stragglers fell out during the march which ranks almost with the subsequent battle of Blenheim to establish Marlborough's reputation.

Now in Bavarian territory, he found the French and their Bavarian allies occupying all the river bridges and had to force a crossing of the Danube at Donauwörth in a pitched battle that cost him 10,000 casualties. On 11 August 1704, Marlborough and Prince Eugène assembled their united army at Tapfheim, not five miles from the strongly fortified Franco-Bavarian camp. Eager to review the enemy position through a telescope, the two men climbed to the top of the village church tower. They had a panoramic view of the fast-flowing River Danube and the nearby village of Blindheim (Blenheim) on the left of the French position, and the low hills and wooded slopes around Lützingen on their right. But between the river and the woods was a broad plain, perhaps four miles wide, made up of cornfields which, at that time of the year, were showing merely stubble after the harvest. In front of the French camp and flowing across the plain towards the Danube was a stream, the Nebel, which made some of the low-lying parts of the plain swampy. Both commanders were highly satisfied with this position as a suitable battlefield, and Marlborough issued instructions for an attack the following day.

The duke had been plagued by a nervous headache in the days leading up to the battle, but when he rose on the morning of battle he felt completely recovered. After prayers he ordered the drums to sound to rouse the soldiers from their sleep and to prepare them for the struggle ahead. In nine columns the Allied troops assembled on the battlefield, numbering about 52,000 men, of whom some 9,000 were British. Closest to Blenheim and the Danube were the British troops under Lord Cutts, known to all as 'the Salamander'. Marlborough commanded the centre, and on the right was Prince

Eugène, with his white-coated Austrian troops, Danes, Hanoverians, and well-drilled Brandenburgers in blue.

The speed of Marlborough's advance had taken the French by surprise. They had expected him to withdraw from what they saw as an untenable position and the thought of him attacking their strong defences never seemed to have occurred. In the French camp soldiers, woken from their sleep, hurried hither and thither seeking their officers, while cavalry squadrons bowled them over and collided with baggage waggons rushing to the rear. Soon order grew out of chaos and the French drummers began to beat out defiance to their opposite numbers, now less than a mile distant. Cannons fired exploratory rounds, and in Blenheim the French defenders knocked holes in the walls of houses to act as loopholes for their muskets. Facing Cutts in the village was the Marquis de Clérambault, while on the far left towards Lützingen was Marshal Marsin with the Elector of Bavaria facing Prince Eugène. Marshal Tallard had taken command of the centre, facing Marlborough himself who, magnificently attired in a scarlet coat and wearing his Order of the Garter, was conspicuous on his white horse. Content with his preparations, the duke dismounted and, in spite of attracting a few shots from the French guns, enjoyed lunch with his senior commanders.

Marlborough's keen eye had seen that the entire French position was hinged at two points – the strongly held villages of Blenheim and Oberglau. Here the French had massed their infantry and, if his proposed counter-attack in the centre was to be successful, Marlborough knew that he would need to keep the garrisons of the two villages fully occupied. He therefore committed his two wings to assaulting the villages and keeping the French busy there. Meanwhile, the Allied soldiers of the centre and left had to stand in silence while the French artillery cut swathes through them. Marlborough had heard nothing from Eugène's right wing to say that it was in position to begin the attack. At last a galloper arrived to say that Eugène was ready and, mounting his horse, Marlborough announced, 'Gentlemen, to your posts!'

The battle was about to begin. Lord Cutts's redcoats marched towards Blenheim, while in the centre the duke's brother Charles was leading the Allied infantry across the swampy ground and into the stream, which, to their surprise, was far more shallow than expected. Incredibly, Tallard – short-sighted but too vain to admit it – could see little of Churchill's attack and gave no orders to check it until the Allied foot were on dry land again. If Charles Churchill was remarkably fortunate, Cutts's English redcoats had run into a storm of French fire outside Blenheim. Clambering over barricades hastily erected by the French defenders, the redcoats fought with sword, bayonet and often musket butt to force their way into the village. But the French fire was overwhelming and over a third of the attackers fell. Next, Lord Orkney directed five more battalions – including the Royal Scots – to force their way into Blenheim.

Tallard was convinced that his right flank, pivoted on Blenheim, could hold for the moment, while on the extreme left Marsin and the Elector were involved in a bloody clinch with Eugène's Austrians and Brandenburgers. Tallard decided to ride to the left to see if Marsin was confident of holding the prince, before returning to deal with Marlborough in the centre. But in his absence, the Marquis de Clérambault made a disastrous decision, the effects of which would help to determine the outcome of the whole battle. Alarmed at the ferocious English assault on Blenheim he ordered first seven battalions from the centre to join the defenders of the village and then, as if that were not enough, a further eleven reserve battalions. Soon over 12,000 French troops were massed in Blenheim, so tightly packed that they could scarcely move; more importantly, they were out of the fight at a time when they were needed in the centre. When the true enormity of his blunder struck the Marquis he rode in anguish into the Danube and drowned himself.

Just as the Allied troops had, not surprisingly, failed to break into Blenheim, so Eugène's men had been bloodily repulsed from Oberglau. The two villages that Marlborough had thought so important to his success were still firmly in French hands. The battle was not going in the way that Marlborough had expected. But generals need to be able to exploit the unexpected. As Tallard watched from his central position, the French heavy cavalry – squadrons of Gendarmes and the men of the King's Household – resplendent in their scarlet coats were riding down the slopes to destroy a line of English dragoons waiting to receive their charge outside Blenheim. It was a mismatch – the English were certain to be overwhelmed by sheer weight of numbers. But nobody had read the script to Colonel Palmes, commanding the five squadrons of dragoons. As the Gendarmes approached, Palmes ordered the dragoons to charge them head-on, and in seconds he had routed the finest cavalry in Europe, sending them reeling back in panic. All along the French line a groan of amazement was heard. The Elector of Bavaria, on the left, could not believe his eyes: 'What! The Gendarmerie fleeing!' It was the turning point of the battle. French confidence sank and Tallard traced his ultimate defeat from that moment.

Outside Oberglau a murderous fight was taking place between the 'Wild Geese', an Irish brigade that fought under the French flag, and ten Allied battalions under the Prince of Holstein-Beck. The Irish gained the upper hand and the prince was killed, but Marlborough refused to give way and kept feeding in men from his centre. There was a crucial moment when Marsin launched sixty squadrons of French horse at Marlborough's flank, but Eugène timed a counter-charge by his Austrian cuirassiers to perfection and the French were scattered. The fighting around Oberglau was confused but terrible in its intensity.

Marlborough was now ready for the great attack that he had been planning from the previous day. The villages of Oberglau and Blenheim were neutralized, and Eugène was holding the Franco-Bavarian left wing in check. The duke now planned to crush the French centre. To do so he had assembled roughly twice the manpower that the French had available, partly through the unwitting assistance of the Marquis de Clérambault, who had isolated so many men uselessly inside the village of Blenheim.

At 5.30 p.m. the trumpets sounded the charge and Marlborough, still conspicuous on his white horse and with his Order of the Garter flashing in the sunlight, led the Allied centre – a mile in width and with 8,000 cavalry and 15,000 infantry – in a massive assault on Tallard's centre. The French tried vainly to hold back the torrent, but they were swept away. Tallard was taken prisoner and the cream of Louis XIV's army routed. Nine French battalions of raw recruits were caught in the open and massacred almost to a man. Robert Parker saw them the next day, 'dead, in rank and file'. One French officer wrote, 'We were borne back on top of one another. So tight was the press that my horse was carried along some three hundred paces without putting hoof to ground right to the edge of a deep ravine.'

The battle was as good as over, though Lord Cutts had an embarrassing time trying to persuade the French masses in Blenheim to surrender. Yet with bluff and a little cunning the thing was done. He ordered the thatched roofs of some nearby cottages to be set alight and then dampened down with water, sending clouds of thick smoke with the wind into Blenheim. The confused French defenders, to the number of some 11,000, came out and surrendered to the far fewer British troops that were engaging them. But the victory had been bought at a high cost. The Allies had lost 4,500 men dead and 7,500 wounded. The French losses were enormous: 38,609 killed, wounded or captured. Once the ferocity of the fighting was over, there was an immediate restoration of eighteenth-century manners. The French commander-in-chief, Marshal Tallard, had been captured by Allied troops. As soon as news reached him, Marlborough sent his personal carriage for Tallard's use. When they later dined together, Tallard remarked, 'I hope your Grace is aware that you have had the honour to defeat the best troops in the world?' Marlborough replied in perfect French, 'Your Lordship, I presume, excepts those who have had the honour to defeat them?'

12

The Battle of Malplaquet
1709

The battle of Malplaquet was the bloodiest battle of the eighteenth century. It is also probably the best example of what is known as a 'Pyrrhic victory', one in which the winning side suffers so much more heavily than the losers that victory seems almost like defeat. Apart from the enormous casualties suffered by the Duke of Marlborough's army at Malplaquet, there was also a nagging feeling that there was no need to have fought the battle at all. Certainly the defeated French had more to celebrate than the British and their allies, and Marlborough's reputation, sky-high after his great victories at Blenheim, Ramillies and Oudenarde, was tarnished. He never fought another battle and his political opponents in Britain ensured that the peace he was striving so hard to win with France in 1709 was not achieved for four more years. Before Malplaquet, France under Louis XIV was facing invasion and defeat; afterwards she achieved survival and recovery. When peace eventually put an end to the War of the Spanish Succession much of Marlborough's work had been undone by lesser men.

During the Allied siege of Mons in 1709, Marlborough and his imperial ally, Prince Eugène of Savoy, found themselves facing a strong French army of 80,000 under Marshals Villars and Boufflers. It was a last desperate effort by the French to save themselves from complete defeat. In fact, the Allies had no need to risk fighting the French at all, particularly as Villars had established so strong a defensive position that he could only be beaten at extreme cost. Marlborough must have realized that the French strategic position would not be much worsened by defeat, yet if they were by some chance to win or even draw a battle it would work wonders to

Death of Tostig and Harold Hardrada after the Battle of Stamford Bridge. A battle which 'brought down the curtain on the Viking Age'.

ABOVE: *Section of the Bayeux Tapestry depicting the Battle of Hastings – perhaps the most important battle in England's history.*

BELOW: *The Battle of Bannockburn. Not since the Battle of Hastings had an English king suffered so complete a defeat.*

The Battle of Crécy – the triumph of the English longbow.

ABOVE: *Joan of Arc paves the way for the final French victory in the Hundred Years War.*

LEFT: *Battle of Agincourt fought by Henry V on 'St Crispin's Day'.*

ABOVE: *Henry VII is crowned at Bosworth – the start of the Tudor dynasty's reign.*

LEFT: *Battle of Towton – the biggest and bloodiest battle ever fought in the British Isles.*

The Earl of Surrey is victorious at Flodden – the most disastrous defeat ever suffered by the Scots.

*Prince Rupert defeated at Marston Moor – the beginning of
the end for King Charles I.*

ABOVE: *Malplaquet – the bloodiest battle of the eighteenth century –
a 'Pyrrhic victory'.*

LEFT: *The Battle of Blenheim – a victory for Marlborough and
the end of French domination in Europe.*

ABOVE: *Culloden Moor – the final encounter in the struggle between the Houses of Hanover and Stuart for the throne of England and Scotland.*

RIGHT: *Clive at the Battle of Plassey. 'Never have such enormous consequences flowed from so tiny a cause.'*

Wolfe is killed during the capture of Quebec from the French. France ceded the whole of Canada to Britain, now 'the greatest maritime and colonial power in the world'.

restore French morale and prestige. Yet the duke's confidence was so high that he never entertained the thought of defeat and hoped to win the war and force the French to accept his terms with one more resounding victory.

Perhaps Marlborough was suffering from hubris. Certainly, commanding an army larger than 110,000, the biggest ever assembled in European history up to that time, was a task beyond even the powers of the most skilled generals like Eugène and Marlborough. As a result, too much authority devolved upon subordinate commanders. And in the case of the brave but foolish Prince of Orange, Marlborough found himself badly served. Just as a century later Wellington found it difficult to rely on his subordinates in Spain, Marlborough faced the old problem that if he wanted something done well he must do it himself. And he could not be everywhere at once, particularly on battlefields that covered many square miles.

The French commander-in-chief, Marshal Villars, had selected an excellent defensive position, amid heavy woods. The only way through the woods was one open stretch, perhaps a mile wide, which was packed with French troops. It was a natural killing ground. Villars was inviting Marlborough to use the tactic of bursting through the centre which had served him so well at Blenheim and Ramillies. Only this time he would pay a terrible price if he attempted it. Marlborough was expecting a substantial addition to his army, no fewer than twenty more battalions under General Withers, marching up from Tournai; so he decided to wait an extra day before attacking, giving the French even more time to turn their wooded position into a veritable fortress.

According to his rank and the number of troops he contributed to the alliance, the Prince of Orange could hardly be denied a senior position in the army, and when Marlborough gave him command of the left wing, facing Marshal Boufflers in the Bois de Lainière, he had every expectation that the more experienced officers around him would be able to control the young man's youthful ardour. Yet the left wing was facing a more difficult task than even Marlborough realized. Boufflers had skilfully positioned twenty cannon in the wood so that they would enfilade the Dutch troops as they advanced. For once the duke's acute observation had failed him.

Marlborough's overall plan of action was to strike the French flanks more or less simultaneously in an effort to persuade Villars to weaken his centre by sending support to his wings. Once the French centre was weakened he would order a general advance and break it with his cavalry. The Allied right wing of Imperial troops under Schulenburg began the assault on the French positions, preceded by an artillery bombardment. But the woods were seething with forty battalions of French troops behind a dense entanglement of branches and chained logs. In the centre the French had palisades of tree trunks and entrenched cannons. To attack these head-on was bound to be suicidal. This was the task of the British troops. Thirty minutes later it was the turn of the left wing to advance. The role of the Prince of Orange's Dutch troops was 'containment' rather than penetration. The problem was that Orange either did not understood this or, piqued at being allocated such a small part in the action, he may have simply disregarded Marlborough's orders. He summoned his thirty Dutch and Scottish battalions and attacked the French positions of De Guiche and D'Artagnan. Twenty cannon poured cannister and grape shot into the Dutch ranks, slaughtering them in a dreadful carnage. Within thirty minutes of going into action, the Prince of Orange, who had two horses killed under him, had suffered over 5,000 casualties. Famous regiments like the Dutch Blue Guards had been almost wiped out.

Meanwhile, on the right, after hard fighting – 7,000 dead carpeted the wood – Schulenburg had broken into the French defences. As Marlborough had expected, Villars had transferred as many as twelve battalions from his centre in an attempt to hold back the assault on his left wing. However, as he surveyed his hard-won gains, the duke received a desperate message telling him to come at once to the left wing where a reverse had been suffered. Both Marlborough and Eugène rode over to the Prince of Orange's headquarters, just in time to prevent the headstrong young man launching a third attack by his ravaged troops. The Dutch had suffered more heavily than any of the Allies in the battle, with 8,600 casualties or 43 per cent of their men involved. It is said that the Dutch state carried the burden of this battle for years to come, with husbands, fathers and sons lost from every important family in the Netherlands.

Nevertheless, the fury of the Dutch attack had caused Villars to send more reinforcements to the aid of Boufflers on his right.

With the French centre weakened, Marlborough now sent thirteen battalions of British troops under Lord Orkney to capture the French redoubts in order to clear the way for his decisive cavalry charge. On such a bloody field it is amazing to relate that these troops decided the issue of the day by occupying the redoubts after finding them virtually empty! So eager had Villars been to strengthen his wings that he had failed to notice that he had virtually abandoned the first line of his centre. Now matters went from bad to worse for the French. No sooner had Orkney taken the redoubts than Villars fell with a bullet in the knee and had to be carried from the field. Command of the French left wing passed to General Puységur, who seemed more concerned to save the army rather than win the battle. He can hardly be blamed, for Marlborough was about to begin his great charge against the French centre with as many as 30,000 horsemen. It was a sight never seen on a battlefield before and possibly never since. Marshal Boufflers tried to stem the flood by bringing his cavalry from the right. He fought like a man demented, turning back the British horse six times but being savaged, in turn, by Orkney's men from the captured redoubts. Suddenly the French army collapsed like a burst balloon. Puységur ordered the French left wing to disengage and retreat, while the French right was finally overrun by the Prince of Orange. Boufflers had no option now but to give way for fear of being encircled. The Allies were so exhausted that they did not pursue the beaten French, who withdrew in good order.

British officers who fought in the centre had never seen such a battle. Lord Orkney wrote, 'In many places [the dead] lie as thick as ever did a flock of sheep. I really think I never saw the like. . . . I hope in God it may be the last battle I may ever see. A very few such would make both parties end the war very soon.' Although the French accepted defeat they had inflicted 25,000 casualties on Marlborough's army at a cost to themselves of some 12,000. Malplaquet was a tragic 'victory' for Marlborough which won him little. It did not even provide him with the peace he wanted. The war dragged on for another four years though Marlborough had one wish – he never commanded another battle.

13

The Battle of Culloden 1746

The era of the Jacobite rebellions, better known as the '15 and '45, was finally brought to an end on a swampy moor about seven miles east of Inverness. The battle fought on Culloden Moor in 1746 marked the final dramatic moment in the struggle between the Houses of Hanover and Stuart for the throne and crown of England and Scotland.

Culloden was the first and the last battle that the Jacobites lost and its aftermath is perhaps more famous and more bitter than the fight itself. Certainly after Culloden the Duke of Cumberland better earned his nickname 'Butcher' than his other cognomen 'Sweet William' and the government displayed an absolute ruthlessness in putting an end once and for all to any threat to the ruling House of Hanover. They had been badly scared by Bonnie Prince Charlie's easy victory at the battle of Prestonpans, in which the English soldiers had fled from the Highlanders 'like rabets'. Moreover, people had flocked to the Jacobite cause throughout Scotland. But time was not on the side of Charles Stuart and by the time his army reached Derby, just 125 miles from London, powerful Hanoverian forces were being assembled against him under General Wade at Newcastle and the Duke of Cumberland, newly returned from Germany, in the west. A retreat to Scotland was the only alternative, which, sullenly, Prince Charles undertook.

Once back in Scotland the Jacobites revived and new recruits joined his cause in thousands. On 17 January 1746, a government army under General Hawley was easily put to flight at Falkirk. Yet, though safe in Scotland, Charles and his advisers realized that they had no chance of securing England without substantial French support.

Meanwhile, the Duke of Cumberland, alarmed by the ease with which the British redcoats had been put to flight by the Highlanders, had been training his troops in anti-Scottish tactics, notably the use of revolving front and rear line so that the Highlanders faced concentrated volley firing, supplemented by an impenetrable hedge of bayonets. Cumberland, the second son of King George II, was a thoroughly unpleasant character and a general of limited abilities. He had been thoroughly outgeneralled by the French Marshal Saxe at Fontenoy, even though the British redcoats had fought with unparalleled bravery in that battle. Nevertheless, though only average on an international stage, Cumberland had more than enough skill to handle Prince Charles's hardy but limited officers.

As Cumberland crossed the border into Scotland the Jacobites fell back before him, hoping to trap him into some indiscretion that they might exploit. But Prince Charles's troops were not prepared for guerrilla warfare. Shortages of money to buy supplies meant that the Jacobites had to scavenge for food, thereby alienating many erstwhile supporters by pillaging their farms. As morale fell Charles Stuart realized that he could not win in the long run. Only an immediate victory over Cumberland could restore support for his cause. He therefore sought a suitable battlefield and instructed his quartermaster-general O'Sullivan to find the right spot. O'Sullivan, unfortunately, failed his prince in every way, selecting the boggy Drummossie Moor, which might hinder the English cavalry but would certainly hinder the Highland charge, which had given them victory in the past.

Although the Jacobites knew that Cumberland was in the vicinity, the English made no attempt to push forward to Drummossie Moor. As a result the Jacobites contrived a daring and risky plan – a night attack on the English camp. It was the last throw of desperate men. But low Scottish morale and the shortage of food hampered the prince's movements. In the first place, a quarter of his men were off looking for food, while others refused to march until they had been fed. In the end some 4,000 men marched off in the darkness, tramping through thick heather and swamp. Soon the army had broken up into bands of lost men and there was no alternative but to turn back and head for Drummossie. But Lord

George Murray in the van reached the English camp. Unfortunately, all he achieved was to raise the alarm and soon English scouts were pursuing the Scottish troops towards the moor. At least now Prince Charles was going to get the battle he wanted.

The Jacobite soldiers assembled on the moor, aware that the redcoats were on their heels. On their right flank stood the so-called Atholl Brigade, commanded by Lord Murray, and consisting mainly of Camerons. Along with them were clansmen of the Stewarts, Mackintoshes and Frasers. In the centre, commanded by Lord John Drummond, were the Farquharsons, while on the left flank stood the Macdonalds. In total there were perhaps 5,000 men. Against them Cumberland opposed perhaps 8,000 redcoats in two lines, the front consisting of the following regiments: Pulteney's, the Royal, Price's, Cholmondeley's, Munro's and Barrel's. The second English line was made up of Howard's, Battereau's, Fleming's, Bligh's, Sempill's, Ligonier's and Wolfe's. Cumberland positioned his artillery in the front line and his cavalry was divided between each flank.

The battle began with a brief artillery duel during which the Jacobites narrowly missed hitting Cumberland himself, a big enough target at eighteen stone, and on a huge grey horse. But the Jacobite guns were soon silenced and for the next thirty minutes Cumberland's guns had complete freedom to slaughter the Scots. This was past enduring and Prince Charles ordered the charge. To general astonishment the Macdonalds on the left refused to move, piqued that they had not been given the point of honour on the right wing. In heavy rain the rest of the Scottish army advanced, but in swampy conditions their charge was hindered. They had hoped that the English redcoats would have been unable to fire because their powder was wet. But Cumberland had taken care that each man had kept his powder dry with his coat lapels. As a result, the Highlanders ran into a heavy volley of gunfire from the redcoats and grapeshot from the cannons. Incredibly, they kept coming and crashed through the English bayonets and soon were engaged in hand-to-hand fighting. But this time the English did not flee like 'rabets'. In fact, many of the redcoats had a score to settle with the Highlanders and the intensity of the struggle was remarkable. No quarter was asked or given and many men died by claymore or bayonet or even spontoon, all the wounds to the front. A soldier in Bligh's regiment reported how his officers fought: 'Some cutting with their swords, others pushing with their spontoons, the sergeants running their halberds into the throats of the enemy, while the soldiers mutually defended each other, ramming their bayonets up to their sockets.' In such a battle, weight of numbers counted for everything and with part of their army refusing to join the fight the Highlanders were doomed. The Macdonalds, stationary from the start of the fight, now threw down their weapons and fled, pursued by the English cavalry.

Cumberland's losses were not heavy, being only 50 dead and 260 wounded. Once the Highlanders broke they were massacred by the Hanoverian cavalry. It was all over in an hour but the aftermath during which Cumberland instigated a reign of terror in the Highlands was to last for many years to come. Prince Charles escaped and hid in the Western Highlands before escaping to France.

14

The Battle of Plassey
1757

The industrial power of Britain in the nineteenth century was based on the treasure of India. In Macaulay's words, the 'workshop of the world' owed much to the 'treasury of Bengal' that was opened to the victor of Plassey, Robert Clive. Certainly industrial and agricultural changes were already taking place in Britain in the mid-eighteenth century and by 1760 the British had made many technological advances, but where was the finance necessary to exploit them? The answer: in the hands of the East India Company and its numerous British investors. Inventors like Cartwright, Hargreaves, Watt and others at last found financial backing for their ideas, and Britain prospered as no other country. As one writer observed, 'It is not too much to say that the destiny of Europe hinged upon the conquest of Bengal.' And this transformation – almost magical in both its cause and effect – was the product of a tiny skirmish at an Indian village where the victors bought their success with the lives of just 23 of their own men and no more than 500 of the enemy.

The decisive struggle between France and Britain in India took place in Bengal. In 1756 the able nawab of Bengal, Alivardi Khan, died and was succeeded by his nephew, Surajah Dowlah. Surajah was disturbed to hear that the British merchants in Calcutta had begun to fortify the city, ostensibly against the threat of a French attack. But Surajah feared that it could be the first step in a British takeover of his land, and warned the merchants that 'if they do not fill up their ditch and raze their fortifications I will expel them totally out of my country'. The British foolishly ignored this warning, and Surajah felt compelled to take action. On 9 May, his

64

troops attacked Calcutta. At first they were driven back by the British defenders, who were vastly outnumbered. Unaware – or dismissive – of European standards in warfare, Surajah then advanced on the British under a flag of truce and overran them, capturing and then imprisoning 145 men in a room designed for just three. In a single torrid night, 121 of the British prisoners died in the appalling crush of the 'Black Hole of Calcutta'. Having committed a crime for which the British would never forgive him, Surajah re-garrisoned Calcutta with 3,000 of his own troops and returned to his capital at Murshidabad, unaware that his actions would trigger a series of events that would topple him from his throne and place his lands under British rule for two centuries.

Returning from a spell of sick leave in England, Lieutenant-Colonel Robert Clive of the army of the East India Company found he had a crisis on his hands. News of the disaster at Calcutta reached Madras in August 1756, and a decision was reached to retake the city and punish Surajah Dowlah for his crimes. Clive was given command of an expeditionary force of 900 British soldiers and 1,500 sepoys, to be ferried to Bengal by a squadron under the command of Admiral Watson. On 31 December, the British fleet reached the mouth of the Ganges and sailed up the River Hooghli. Under cover of the ships' guns, the 39th Foot, led by Captain Eyre Coote, stormed into Calcutta and took the city at the cost of just a handful of wounded.

Clive then received news that Britain and France were at war once again in Europe. This – the start of the Seven Years' War – changed the strategic situation. The French had 300 troops with artillery at Chandernagore and, in the event of a British attack on the nawab, it was predictable that the French would come to Surajah's aid. In any case, on hearing of Clive's arrival, Surajah had raised an army of 40,000 men and was advancing on Calcutta. On 3 February, just outside the city, Clive launched a surprise attack on the Bengalis at dawn. At first all was confusion and the British suffered 150 casualties but at last the Indians were defeated and Surajah agreed to make peace with the British. On 9 February, Surajah agreed to reinstate the merchants of the Company in Calcutta.

But Clive already had other things on his mind. War with France freed him to attack the French base at Chandernagore, which he succeeded in taking by assault on 14 March. News of this enraged Surajah Dowlah who, fearing the British were becoming too strong in Bengal, opened negotiations with the Marquis de Bussy, the French commander in the Carnatic. Both Clive and Admiral Watson were now convinced that Surajah could not be trusted and looked for a way to remove him from power. Events played into their hands. Unlike his uncle of fond memory, Surajah was regarded by his people as a cruel, debauched tyrant, who had inflamed the hatred of a group of his nobles, led by his commander-in-chief, Mir Jafar. The conspirators saw in Clive the means by which the nawab might be deposed. They approached Clive and admiral Watson in Calcutta to ask if the British would support their plot to overthrow Surajah. Clive – with a ruthlessness that marked him as closer to the empire-builders of the sixteenth and seventeenth centuries than to those of his own time – replied that he would. In return for control of all French trading posts and settlements in Bengal, possession of Calcutta and its environs, and compensation for the 'Black Hole' atrocity, Clive promised to place Mir Jafar on the throne of Bengal.

Clive advanced on Surajah's capital at Murshidabad, his force swelled to 900 British, 200 half-caste Portuguese, 2,100 sepoys and 10 artillery pieces. But how much trust could he place on the word of Mir Jafar? Clearly, if things went badly, Mir Jafar, for all his oaths and protestations, would stay loyal to the nawab. In fact, within days a message arrived for Clive from Mir Jafar, still professing loyalty to the British but indicating that he hoped to stay neutral in the coming fight. Undeterred, Clive moved his small army across the River Baggiruttee and reached the small village of Plassey on 23 June. The British soldiers took refuge in a grove of mango trees and tried to get some sleep, but found their slumbers disturbed by the appalling cacophony made by the drums and cymbals of the nawab's approaching army.

The next day, Surajah deployed his whole army in a huge arc around the small British force, apparently trapping it in the mango grove. A total of 35,000 Bengali infantry and 18,000 cavalry, with 50 guns pulled by oxen and pushed into position by elephants, some covered in metal armour, faced Clive's miniscule force of just 3,200. In addition, a small group of French soldiers had joined the nawab with four extra field guns. To Surajah it must have seemed like a good day for a massacre. To Clive, who was viewing the scene from the roof of a hunting lodge alongside the river, it must have seemed like a good day for a miracle.

Clive decided that boldness was the best policy. He marched his entire force out and lined them up facing the enemy division commanded by the nawab's only really loyal officer, Mir Muddin. He concluded that if he could win here, other commanders – notably Mir Jafar – would almost certainly give up the fight. The firing began when the French opened up with their light guns and the British replied, silencing them in a short time. But soon the full arc of Surajah's army was firing at the British and, after just thirty minutes' combat and a mere 30 men injured, Clive retired his men behind the walls of the mango orchard, telling them to keep their heads down. Meanwhile, the British gunners were firing through holes cut in the wall of the orchard and were scything down the nawab's men in hundreds. Still the Bengalis refused to advance, and Clive decided to wait under cover until nightfall and then attack the enemy camp. It was at that moment that the miracle that Clive had been waiting for occurred. Seemingly out of a clear sky a rainstorm swept the entire area. The British, sheltering under tarpaulins in the orchard, kept their weapons and powder dry, but out in the open the nawab's army was drenched and the fire of their cannons fizzled out. Mir Muddin chose this moment to charge towards the orchard, but was hit by a torrent of grapeshot and killed, whereupon his men panicked and fled.

Surajah now called on Mir Jafar for advice. Mir Jafar could hardly credit his luck. Advising the nawab to leave the field and return to his capital, he promised to 'mop up' the British troops for him. As Surajah left the field, Mir Jafar sent a message to Clive suggesting that he should attack now and the day would be his. Whether he needed this advice is a moot point, for Clive took the initiative and brought his troops back into the open. The Bengali army was now leaderless – with the nawab fled, Mir Muddin dead and Mir Jafar a traitor – and Clive was able to rake their ranks with grapeshot and massed musketry. By 5.00 p.m. the British had taken Surajah's camp and the battle was over. Clive had looked for a miracle, and it had happened: 3,000 men had put to flight 50,000.

The next morning the slippery Mir Jafar came into camp to congratulate Clive on his victory. Clive welcomed him as the new ruler of Bengal, and the former nawab was pursued by Mir Jafar's son and executed in cold blood. Clive reached Murshidabad on 29 June, officially installing the new nawab. He was soon seen – as Clive had always intended it – as a puppet of the East India Company, with a British resident at court guiding his hand.

Never have such enormous consequences flowed from so tiny a cause. The battle of Plassey was no more than a skirmish, and the British victory was earned less by the fighting qualities of the British troops than by the indomitable willpower of Robert Clive, who had the courage to outface a force nearly twenty times his own in size. Nor must the treachery of Mir Jafar be forgotten. Without his 'help' it is possible that the British could have lost the battle and with it their hold on Bengal. And from this skirmish both political and economic advantages flowed: the Company became landlords of the 'twenty-four Parganas' – 900 square miles of land around Calcutta – which yielded fabulous wealth in rents. With Warren Hastings as resident at the court of Murshidabad the British were supreme in Bengal; and with such power the nature of the East India Company undertook a significant change. From a company of merchants emerged a powerful political force that was to govern large parts of India for the next hundred years.

15

The Fall of Quebec 1759

During the Seven Years' War Britain's prime minister, William Pitt ('the elder'), was convinced that the French empire in North America was breaking up. Vastly outnumbered by the British colonies to the south – French Canada had a population of just 82,000 against the 13 British colonies with 1,300,000 – and surrounded by enemies on all sides, the French colonies were abandoned to their fate by the mother country, which was facing severe problems of its own in Europe. But the French commanders in Canada, Louis Antoine de Bougainville and Louis de St Véran, Marquis de Montcalm, were not the kind of men to give up easily. At Ticonderoga the previous year, Montcalm – greatly outnumbered – had crushed a clumsy assault by the British general, Abercrombie, and unless the British could find better commanders, Montcalm was confident of holding his bases along the St Lawrence River against whatever the British could send.

By 1759 William Pitt devised an ambitious three-fold assault on Canada. While General Amherst was to capture Ticonderoga and Crown Point on Lake Champlain, General Prideaux was to take Fort Niagara, sail down Lake Ontario, and capture Montreal. But the main strike was to be against Quebec on the St Lawrence River, and was to be carried out by the brilliant but unorthodox 32-year-old General James Wolfe, son of one of Marlborough's veterans. Wolfe was a frail-looking man who suffered from tuberculosis and kidney problems, but his eyes burned with a furious intensity. Wolfe it was who gave rise to George II's most celebrated saying: when told by jealous rivals that Wolfe was mad, the king replied, 'Mad is he? Well, I wish he would bite some of my other generals.' The death of Wolfe at Quebec undoubtedly robbed his country of a brilliant commander who might have made all the difference in the later War of American Independence.

Wolfe left England aboard the *Neptune* on 14 February 1759, with a fleet of 70 ships under Admiral Saunders, and by May the force that was to assault Quebec was assembling at Louisbourg, in the Gulf of St Lawrence. There were to be 8,500 regular British troops under young brigadiers chosen by Wolfe himself: one observer called it 'a boy's campaign', but it was not going to be child's-play. Quebec was a powerfully fortified town on a rocky headland, hundreds of feet above the St Lawrence, and defended by a garrison of 14,000 men with 106 guns. Montcalm was confident that any British attack would have to be made on the eastern side of the town and he dug his trenches and gun emplacements there, between the Beauport and St Charles Rivers, manning them with the majority of his men. But the French had grounds for additional confidence. It was believed by the best French naval opinion that the St Lawrence could not be navigated beyond Quebec without great risk. However, Wolfe was blessed with seamen of unusual quality, and one young officer, James Cook – later of even greater fame than his general – took soundings and mapped the river so accurately that his work was not superseded for a hundred years. The local pilots felt it was an impossible task for such ships, but they had reckoned without British captains like one known as old Killick.

Aboard Killick's transport, *Goodwill*, one enraged Canadian pilot vowed that Canada would be the graveyard of the British army and the walls of Quebec would be hung with English scalps. Captain Killick, angrily pushed the Canadian aside and went forward to the forecastle to guide the ship through himself. The pilot shouted that the ship would be wrecked for no French ship had ever attempted the traverse without a pilot. 'Aye, aye, my dear,' old Killick shouted back, fiercely shaking his speaking-trumpet, 'but damn me, I'll convince you that an Englishman shall go where a Frenchman dare not show his nose.' Behind *Goodwill* the captain of the following ship was alarmed to learn that *Goodwill* had no pilot. 'Who's your master?' he yelled, and Killick replied, 'It's old Killick, and that's enough.'

Leaning over the bow the old man chatted gaily with the soldiers in the sounding boats, giving his orders easily while pointing out the different shades of blue and grey indicating the depth of the water, warning of submerged ridges marked by telltale ripples or the sudden disturbance of smoothly flowing waters. Eventually *Goodwill* emerged from the zig-zag traverse into easier water. Killick put down his trumpet and handed the ship over to his mate. 'Well, damn me,' he snorted, 'damn me if there are not a thousand places in the Thames more hazardous than this. I'm ashamed that Englishmen should make such a rout about it.' Such men were at the root of England's successes during the eighteenth century.

Having successfully landed his troops at Île d'Orléans, Wolfe initially agreed with the views of his opposite number, that the best way to attack Quebec was from the east. But he soon recognized that this was exactly where the French wanted him to attack and that Montcalm had a powerful force dug in there. After weeks of scanning Quebec through a telescope Wolfe was rescued from his dilemma by the Royal Navy. On 18 July some ships, including the *Sutherland*, penetrated the river beyond Quebec. Montcalm was horrified, realizing now the possibility that a landing could be made to the south of the town. To cover this he sent troops under Bougainville to patrol this area. It was a battle of wits between two able generals, each praying that the enemy would succumb to hunger before his own troops did. From his study of the area Wolfe concluded that there was only one possible place where he could force the French to give battle in the open, away from their massive defences to the east, and that was the Plains of Abraham, to the south of the city, named after a French sailor who had once owned the land. The problem was that the only way to reach the plains was by scaling a cliff that towered 200 feet above the river.

On further investigation, Wolfe learned that there was a path to the top of the cliff, so with a force of 4,500 men, he set off in a series of longboats to follow behind the *Sutherland*, which was showing just two lamps at her stern. The first boat carried Wolfe with 24 light infantry who would make the first ascent. Behind came 1,300 men from Monckton's and Murray's brigades. In the second wave came 1,910 men of Townshend's brigade, with 1,200 men kept in reserve. During the slow and dark journey down the river Wolfe was heard to recite Gray's *Elegy*, surprising everyone with the admission that he would rather have written that poem than take Quebec. He repeated the poet's last line with emphasis, 'The paths of glory lead but to the grave.'

French sentries patrolling the beach noticed the dark shapes on the river. *'Qui vive?'* called one. A Highland officer, Captain Donald McDonald, replied in perfect French, *'La France.' 'Quel régiment?'* enquired the guard. *'De Reine,'* said McDonald, naming one of Bougainville's regiments. Satisfied, the sentry returned to his patrol. At 4.00 a.m. the British boats reached the beach below the cliff. The beach was deserted. Clearing away the tree trunks and bracken with which the French had concealed the path, the British troops, with their Indian scouts, began clambering up towards the top of the cliff. The whole operation had been a triumph for the navy, which had negotiated a difficult river in almost total darkness and delivered its human cargo safely to its destination.

Within two hours the full complement of 4,828 men were on the heights. But Wolfe knew there was no time to waste. He must bring Montcalm to battle before the Frenchman could assemble his full strength. Wolfe's final orders to his assault troops have the ring of Nelson about them: 'A vigorous blow struck at this juncture may determine the fate of Canada . . . The officers and men will remember what their country expects from them, and what a determined body of soldiers inured to war are capable of doing.'

The French officer who should have been guarding the Anse de Foulon, where the British came ashore, had been so confident that it was impossible for a landing to be made there that he had carelessly dismissed forty of his men to help with the harvesting at a nearby village. While he slept the impossible had happened.

For perhaps the only time in his life Montcalm panicked. The last thing he had expected was to see British troops fully drawn up for battle on the Plains of Abraham. With just 5,000 of the town's garrison he hastened out to give battle, not giving Bougainville time to join him with a further 3,000 front-line troops. Both sides opened fire at long range and Wolfe was hit in the wrist, but not incapacitated. As the lines of British and French troops advanced towards each other, it was noticeable that the British were proving steadier. At just 50 yards the British stopped and, when ordered, fired what was, according to Sir John Fortescue, 'the most perfect [volley] ever fired on any battlefield, which burst forth as if from a single monstrous weapon, from end to end of the British line'. The result was shattering – and the French had no chance to recover as the redcoats and Highlanders hurled themselves upon their enemies. As Wolfe led the 28th Foot into the fray he was shot first in the groin and then soon afterwards through the lungs. Desperate that his men should not see him fall, he asked an officer to support him. Carried to the rear, he lived just long enough to hear a soldier shout, 'See how they run.' 'Who run?' enquired Wolfe. 'The enemy, sir,' replied the soldier. 'Now God be praised, I will die in peace,' murmured Wolfe, as he slipped into a coma from which he did not awake.

Less than a mile away a similar tragedy was being enacted. Montcalm, mounted and attempting to rally his troops, was shot through the body and only held in his saddle by an aide. Riding back into Quebec so that no one should see that he was hit, the brave French general did not even have the consolation of victory that had eased Wolfe's passing. He lingered painfully, only dying the following morning. He was buried in a British shell hole in the Ursuline Convent in Quebec.

But the battle was not yet over. With the main actors removed from the scene, it was up to the supporting cast to consolidate the British gains. The French, had they but known it, still had a substantial numerical advantage. But Brigadier Townshend never let them settle long enough to regroup. If Wolfe was the victor on the Plains of Abraham, it was Townshend who captured Quebec. The battle ended with the British having lost just 630 casualties and the French 830. After all the blood that had been spilled in the previous hundred years of Anglo-French warfare in North America it was incredible that the future of Canada should have been decided so cheaply. On the afternoon of 17 September, the French flag was lowered in the citadel of Quebec to be replaced by the Union Flag.

The Treaty of Paris in 1763 finally put the stamp of legality on the work of Wolfe and his redcoats at Quebec. France ceded to Britain the whole of Canada. In the words of Chateaubriand, 'France has disappeared from North America like those Indian tribes with which she sympathized.' The future lay with Britain, which was now 'the greatest maritime and colonial power in the world'.

16

The Battle of Minden
1759

The British redcoated infantryman of the eighteenth century was a remarkable soldier. In media terms he has had a bad press. In Scotland he is seen as a persecutor of the Highland clans – in Hollywood terms the enemy of Rob Roy McGregor. In the United States he is the brutal oppressor of American liberties and the enemy in the War of Independence. With his over-fussy eighteenth-century uniform, his tricorn hat, leather stock and powdered wig he is sometimes seen as effete, or at least hardly a match for the American woodsman or Indian warrior. The truth, of course, is very different. The British redcoat was very much a creature of eighteenth-century European warfare, modelled on the Prussian soldiers of King Frederick William I of Prussia and his brilliant son, Frederick the Great. He was drilled to become part of a unit of concentrated firepower, not an individual. The massed armies of European wars required little initiative on the part of their soldiers. The more a man thought, the more he fell prey to his fears. No thinking man would willingly stand upright no more than thirty paces from the enemy, exchanging musket fire until he fell, or stand ready to receive bayonet thrusts from the enemy infantry or sabre slashes from the passing cavalry. A thinking man would look for cover, or for a way of escape. And once a soldier thought of how to preserve his own life his efficiency became suspect.

On 1 August 1759, the British redcoats – derisively called 'bloodybacks' by the Americans for their frequent floggings – achieved at Minden one of the most heroic and extraordinary victories in recorded history. The battle was, for Britain, one of the most significant battles of the eighteenth century. Politically, it was a battle fought to save Hanover from being overrun by the French, but militarily it contained two incidents representing the extremes of the military spectrum.

At Minden there occurred one of the most famous acts of cowardice in military history when the commander of the British cavalry, Lord George Sackville, refused to obey a direct order to attack from the commander-in-chief, the Duke Ferdinand of Brunswick, for which he was later court-martialled and driven out of the service. When Sackville received the orders to charge the fleeing French and ensure a great victory, he sat stock still and did nothing. Three times the order was repeated by different aides but each time Sackville claimed he did not understand it. When his deputy, the Marquis of Granby, tried to respond to Ferdinand's order and lead out the second line of cavalry, Sackville stopped him and the French managed to escape. King George II was furious, court-martialling him on a charge of cowardice and cashiering him from the army with the heavy sentence that he should never again serve the king in any capacity whatsoever. Sackville was lucky not to be shot; Admiral Byng had been executed for far less.

The battle also contained an episode of almost suicidal bravery by the British infantry who, though outnumbered many times over, attacked the massed French cavalry and drove it off the field. So astonishing, even unprecedented, was this action that the French commander, the Marquis Louis de Contades, remarked, 'I have seen what I never thought to be possible – a single line of infantry break through three lines of cavalry ranked in order of battle and tumble them to ruin.'

The French army numbered some 60,000 men with 162 guns, while the Anglo-German army of the Duke of Brunswick fielded just 45,000 with 170 guns. The right of Brunswick's army comprised six British infantry regiments – the 12th (Napier's), 20th (Kingsley's), 23rd (Hulke's), 25th (Howe's), 37th (Stuart's) and the 51st (Brudenell's) – as well as a Hanoverian regiment, all under the command of Lieutenant-General von Spoercken. It was formed in two lines: the first – under Waldegrave – consisted of the 12th, 37th and 23rd, and the second – under Kingsley – of the 20th, 51st and 25th. The regiments averaged only about 500 men each at the start of the action.

Like the infamous 'Charge of the Light Brigade' a century later at Balaclava, the drama at Minden began with a misunderstood order. But rarely could a mix-up have had a better or more extraordinary outcome. At just after dawn on 1 August, one of the Duke of Brunswick's aides arrived at General von Spoercken's headquarters with the order that he was to advance at the 'sound of the drum'. There was nothing unusual in this, for coordinating troops on an eighteenth-century battlefield was frequently carried out by drumbeat. All Brunswick was saying was that when he wanted the British infantry to advance he would signal them by a drumcall. Incredibly, when von Spoercken passed the message to the British general Waldegrave, speaking in French as was the custom at the time, Waldegrave mistranslated what his commander had said and thought he meant that the British must advance 'to the sound of the drum', meaning that they would advance immediately with drums beating. At once Waldegrave ordered his drummers to sound the advance and the first British line set off towards the French. The second line was amazed to find their colleagues marching away and promptly set off after them. Observing from far off the splendid sight of the perfectly aligned troops in their white gaiters, red jackets and black tricorn hats, Brunswick raged and fumed. He could see his chances of victory being thrown away. Any moment the French artillery would tear the British lines to shreds. And for a while this is exactly what seemed to be happening. While the two lines of infantry headed straight towards the French cavalry in the centre of the French army, the French gunners, backed up by regiments of infantry, poured a deadly fire into them.

Rarely can firmness and resolution have been in greater demand. Yet, the fighting spirit of the soldiers seemed to increase at every step. As dozen after dozen of redcoats were literally torn to pieces by the gunfire the men never wavered or hurried, yet within them was the urge to strike back at their tormenters. As one of them wrote, 'The soldiers, so far from being daunted by their falling comrades, breathed nothing but revenge.'

All this time the French cavalry commander, General Fitzjames, had been watching the two lines of infantry approach, at any moment expecting them to break under the deluge of shot and shell that had been hitting them. But, puzzlingly, they continued to advance towards him without even attempting to form squares, the normal defence when faced with cavalry. Lines of infantry had never before been known to stand against cavalry. Fitzjames had 63 squadrons of cavalry drawn up in three lines and he ordered the first line – 11 squadrons under the Marquis de Castrie – to put an end to the impudent Englishmen. To the sound of trumpets the French cavalry rode down on the two red lines ahead of them. At the head of the first, Waldegrave calmly ordered his men to prepare to fire. Not until the horsemen were within ten paces did the order to fire ring out. Fire discipline, under the trying circumstances, could well have been ragged. But on this occasion the men fired as one and the French cavalry was shattered as if it had ridden into a brick wall. Hundreds of men and horses were downed in a split second and soon the front of the British line was a sea of writhing horses and screaming men. Even the British officers were horrified at the effect of such a volley at such short range. Thompson wrote, 'such a terrible fire that not even lions could have come on, such a number of them fell, both horses and men, that it made it difficult for those not touched to retire.'

In the French ranks a cry of both anger and amazement went up as the remnants of the cavalry veered away from the enemy; it was Crécy and Agincourt rolled into one. Now the second line of cavalry – an even bigger force – rode out to replace their worsted comrades. Brunswick saw that the only chance of saving the infantry and perhaps even saving the battle was for Lord Sackville to lead out the British cavalry while the French were disordered. As we have seen, Sackville refused to do so. While he argued with Brunswick's aides and found reason after reason for not obeying orders, the redcoats prepared to meet fourteen squadrons of fresh French horsemen. But the ground in front of the British lines was made impassable by the bodies of wounded and dead men and horses. Nevertheless, pride and shame drove the Frenchmen for-ward, but again the redcoats timed their volley to perfection and routed the horsemen at point-blank range. By now almost half of the entire French cavalry had been defeated by the first line of just three British regiments. The spirit of Waldegrave's soldiers was sky-high. They believed that they could do anything, perhaps even beat the whole French army on their own. However, Contades had decided to put a stop to the whole charade. While 1,500 elite troopers under the Marquis de Poyanne charged the front of the British line, he ordered his infantry to attack each flank at the same time. The British would be overwhelmed by sheer weight of numbers.

If Sackville and the British cavalry were prepared to watch their comrades overwhelmed, the same could not be said of the British artillery, who chose this moment to enter the fray. Captain Macbean, with ten heavy guns, sized up the situation at a glance. As he put it, 'They were going to gallop down, sword in hand, among our poor mangled regiments, but we clapt our matches to the ten guns and gave them such a salute as they little expected: for we mowed them down like standing corn.' Poyanne's Gendarmes had veered towards the Hanoverians, who had advanced alongside the British. But here they received as rough treatment as from the British regiments and soon hundreds of them were unhorsed. The French cavalry had been beaten more completely than on any field in anyone's memory and by infantry, who simply refused to be beaten. Yet even now von Spoercken's invincible infantry were not finished. Having dealt the cavalry a mortal blow, they now faced the advancing French infantry. First the 12th and 37th Regiments routed the Régiments de Condé, Aquitaine and du Roi. As Montgomery explained succinctly: 'We killed a good many and the rest ran away.' Next a regiment of Saxon Grenadiers (Saxony was in alliance with France at this time) fell on the depleted ranks of the 12th and 37th. Montgomery described what followed: 'As fine and terrible-looking fellows as I ever saw. They stood us a tug, notwithstanding they beat us off a distance, where they galled us much, they having rifled barrels, and our muskets would not reach them. To remedy this we advanced; they took the hint and ran away.' Finally when more Saxons attacked, Spoercken decided it was time to use his second line, which was commanded by General Kingsley. Kingsley's three regiments had suffered the frustration of not being able to do much more than suffer casualties without striking back at their assailants. They soon put that to rights by shattering the remaining Saxon infantry and driving them pell-mell from the field.

Robbed of what might have been one of the most complete victories in history by Lord Sackville's refusal to commit the cavalry to the contest, Brunswick had to be content with the partial victory that the British infantry had given him. Contades withdrew his army, having suffered 7,000 casualties in dead and wounded as well as 5,000 prisoners. His cavalry had been so savaged by von Spoercken's redcoats that the French Foreign Minister, the Duc de Choiseul later wrote, 'The thought of Minden makes me blush for the French army.'

17

The Battle of Saratoga
1777

Luck and geography are the supreme fortunes in the history of a nation. While the Channel has served on innumerable occasions to prevent the marauding hordes of one European conqueror after another from trampling the lawns of England's 'green and pleasant land', the broad width of the Atlantic Ocean in 1776 stood between Britain's American rebels and the retribution of the mother-country. Yet even more than this natural advantage, the Americans enjoyed remarkable luck. During the Seven Years' War British generals and admirals had won victory after victory, men like Wolfe, Clive and Hawke adding lustre to the British cause in the far-flung parts of the world. Yet with Wolfe dead at Quebec and future giants like Horatio Nelson, John Moore and Arthur Wellesley years away from command, the British Army was undergoing a low point in its history at precisely the time when it was most needed to suppress the American colonials. Instead of meeting the Iron Duke with his veterans from Spain as they would have done a mere generation later, the colonials were to be confronted by German mercenaries under the command of men like the vain playwright general 'Gentleman Johnny' Burgoyne, whom Horace Walpole astutely dubbed 'Julius Caesar Burgonius'. And in the trough between elder and younger Pitt, colonial policy was the product of minds of little talent, notably that of Secretary for the Colonies, Lord George Germain, coward of Minden.

General Burgoyne began his march from Canada on 31 June, with a force of 7,213 regulars, comprising three brigades of British and three of Hessians and Brunswickers. In addition, he took 250 Canadians and American loyalists, as well as about 500 Indians. It was a colourful display, with the red coats of the British line regiments and the blue of the Germans standing out sharply against the background of the Canadian forests. Keeping a diary of the expedition was the redoubtable Baroness von Riedesel, wife of the Brunswick general, with her three young daughters.

The first part of the journey was by boat on the glistening waters of Lake Champlain, with the Indians in their brightly-painted birchbark canoes leading the way for the armada and Burgoyne and his fellow generals, Phillips and Riedesel, following in their pinnaces. As a display of British naval might it was impressive, but the expedition was ill-prepared for the march overland: once the lake was passed, the lack of carts and wagons made for painful progress. As an ominous warning the column was frequently interrupted by heavy storms, which were followed by a plague of black flies.

As a diversion, Burgoyne had sent Colonel Barry St Leger with 875 regulars via the St Lawrence River to Fort Oswego, on Lake Ontario, where he met 1,000 Indians under the brilliant, English-educated Mohawk chief, Joseph Brant. It was proposed that St Leger would first take Fort Stanwix before marching down the Mohawk Valley to join Burgoyne before Albany. Burgoyne had hoped the appearance of British troops would encourage loyalists to rise in his support; in fact, he was quite wrong and the sight of so many Indians had the reverse effect, with settlers thronging to join the rebel militias.

Burgoyne's main column reached Fort Ticonderoga on 1 July. The fort was held for the rebels by Major-General St Clair with just 2,500 troops, but the size of the British force persuaded St Clair to abandon his post and retreat to Fort Edward. Although Burgoyne was just 70 miles from Albany and could have continued by water to Fort George, just a short march from the Hudson River, he allowed himself instead to be persuaded to march his troops overland from Skenesboro, apparently on the advice of loyalist major Philip Skene. Skene's advice was not entirely disinterested: the building of a road through the wild terrain by the British troops would link his colony with the Hudson and improve his trade once the war was over. The American general Schuyler used scorched-earth tactics to delay the British advance, cutting down thousands of trees and even damming and redirecting streams across their path. Swarms of mosquitoes rose from the swamps to attack the suffering British soldiers, adding to the misery of the hundreds already suffering from dysentery. In fact, Burgoyne wasted three weeks in completing a march that should have taken a matter of days. His supply line stretched over 150 miles back to Montreal and food was becoming short. Short of horses and wagons, Burgoyne sent back appeals to Montreal for help.

Burgoyne desperately needed mounts for his dragoons, for without horses they were just a liability. Hearing that there was a plentiful supply of horses near Bennington in Vermont, Burgoyne sent Colonel Baum with a force of 500 men, including 150 of the Brunswickers, to collect the horses and whatever stores they could find. The raid was supposed to be conducted with stealth, yet the Germans marched off behind their regimental bands playing patriotic tunes. After being harassed by snipers on the march, Baum sent back to Burgoyne for reinforcements and a further 650 men under Colonel von Breymann were sent. Warned that there was a force of 1,500 New Hampshire militia in the area, commanded by General John Stark, Burgoyne dismissed the threat as insignificant.

On 16 August Stark infiltrated Baum's column by disguising some of his men as loyalists with white paper badges in their hats. Roaring 'There, my boys, are your enemies. You must beat them, or Molly Stark is a widow tonight,' his troops drove off the loyalists and Indians, killed Baum, and wiped out most of his force. Breymann arrived with his reinforcements only to be set upon by Stark's triumphant militia, who inflicted a further 230 casualties on the Germans before sending them scattering.

Meanwhile, many miles away to the west, St Leger's column had moved down the Mohawk Valley and besieged Fort Stanwix, which was held by 750 Americans under Peter Gansevoort and Marinus Willet. An American relief force of 800 New York Militia, led by General Nicholas Herkimer, was ambushed by Mohawk Indians under Joseph Brant at Oriskany and badly cut up. Herkimer was wounded early in the fighting but was propped up against a tree and, continuing to smoke his pipe contentedly, gave orders to the last. Eventually Brant called off his Indians, leaving the remnants of Herkimer's force to withdraw. When news of this setback reached General Schuyler at Stillwater he sent Benedict Arnold with a further 900 men to relieve the fort.

To effect the relief of Fort Stanwix Benedict Arnold used a clever trick, sending into the Indian camp a half-witted Dutchman named Hon-Yost Schuyler to spread rumours that a huge American force was advancing towards them. The Indians regarded half-wits as being in touch with the spirit Manitou, so when Hon-Yost pointed at the leaves of the trees to indicate the American numbers, they abandoned the siege and deserted, leaving St Leger with such a depleted force that he had no option but to pull back to Canada. Burgoyne's situation was now hopeless, with his western force in retreat and his German troops decimated, but with the desperation of an inveterate gambler he decided to push on towards Albany, where he hoped to be able to winter his army.

Burgoyne decided to march his depleted force of 7,000 men down the west side of the Hudson River, crossing over a bridge of boats and bringing it into direct confrontation with the Americans. Congress had blamed Schuyler for the loss of Ticonderoga and had replaced him with Gates, an ex-British regular officer, known to Burgoyne as 'the old midwife'. Midwife or not, Gates had taken up a strong defensive position on Bemis Heights, near the village of Saratoga, and Washington had reinforced him with Colonel Daniel Morgan's corps of buckskin-clad sharpshooters from Virginia and west Pennsylvania. Morgan was a gnarled veteran of Braddock's fateful expedition to the Monongahela in 1755 and still bore the scars of the five hundred lashes he had once received for striking a British officer. His light infantry, often fighting stripped to the waist, Indian style, were reputed to be able to sever a squirrel's tail at a hundred paces with their long-barrelled flintlock rifles.

The British assaulted the American position on 19 September in what became known as the battle of Freeman's Farm, with the Brunswick general Riedesel commanding the British left, Burgoyne and Hamilton the centre, and the Scottish general Fraser the right. Fraser's advance guard was decimated by Morgan's impetuous sharpshooters, but the Americans were too eager and were hit and scattered by a volley from Hamilton's brigade, leaving their commander in tears and trying to regroup his men with his famous turkey call. Heavy fighting around Freeman's Farm involved a see-saw struggle, with the Americans seizing the British guns but being driven back at the point of the bayonet, while American snipers in the trees shot down the majority of the British officers, easily identified by their gorgets and epaulets. But the Americans missed the chance of striking a decisive blow when Gates refused Benedict Arnold the men he needed to break Burgoyne's centre. The British commander called on Riedesel to bring up men and guns, and by the late afternoon the Brunswick artillery was firing grapeshot into the quivering American ranks. At last Gates was forced to pull back his men, leaving the British victorious but bloodied, having lost over 600 men to the Americans' 300.

Burgoyne had gained little by this Pyrrhic victory and retired to lick his wounds. With starvation a real possibility, and with packs of wolves roving at night to dig up the recently buried corpses, Burgoyne now overrode the advice of his generals – who favoured retreat – and decided on another attack on the American position at Bemis Heights on 7 October. This time the attack would be spearheaded by just 1,600 men – a desperate move, even for this reckless commander.

Meanwhile, a bitter row had broken out in the American camp between the two senior American officers, causing Gates to dismiss his most able commander, 'that son-of-a-bitch' Arnold. However, Arnold was not to be removed so easily and a round-robin among the other American generals urged him to stay in camp. No sooner had the fighting begun than Arnold rode out of the camp to the cheers of his men, pursued by one of Gates's aides with orders for him to return. Conscious of the effectiveness of the famous Scottish officer, Simon Fraser, Arnold ordered a backwoods sharpshooter, Tim Murphy, to pick him off. Fraser was undismayed by Murphy's first two near-misses and, mounted on a white horse, continued leading his men. However, Murphy's third shot hit its mark. With Fraser mortally wounded, British resistance faded. Arnold seemed to be everywhere, 'more like a madman than a cool and discreet officer', racing from one end of the battle to the other, leading assaults, overriding other generals' orders and capturing Breymann's redoubt, before being shot in the thigh and carried from the field. If any one man's example won the fight that day it was Benedict Arnold's.

Burgoyne withdrew, having suffered 600 losses to 150 by the Americans. The weather was appalling – it rained incessantly and his men were exhausted by battle and by lack of food. Burgoyne now retired with the utmost secrecy to a fortified camp at Saratoga. For a while Burgoyne tried to drive away thoughts of his predicament by carousing with plundered liquor at the captured mansion of General Schuyler at Fishkill.

But there was to be no happy ending for Burgoyne and his army, and on 17 October he surrendered his remaining 5,000 troops and their stores to Gates, who offered generous terms, allowing the British to march out with the honours of war. Yet although Burgoyne was permitted to return to Britain on parole, his defeat at the battle of Saratoga was 'a thunderclap, which resounded round the world'. The American Congress adopted the Articles of Confederation, strengthening the national feeling of the 13 separate colonies. In the long run this was to prove a decisive event in American history.

18

The Battle of Albuera
1811

The Duke of Wellington's description of his own troops is rightly famous: 'the scum of the earth.' Yet he knew that for all their character faults there were no troops like them. The French certainly knew what they were up against. In the aftermath of the battle of Albuera, Marshal Soult wrote to Napoleon, 'There is no beating these troops. They were completely beaten, the day was mine, and they did not know it and would not run away.' It was perhaps Napoleon's good fortune that he never met these troops in battle. Soult had told him that *l'infanterie anglaise en duel, c'est le diable.'*

Wellington's 'Peninsular veterans' were a special breed. In general they were the 'restless spirits' among the British lower classes, men who could not settle to a job and who would have as readily turned to crime as to the armed services if matters had taken a different turn. The Duke of Wellington would never have believed that his soldiers enlisted from feelings of personal pride or honour, although there is evidence that this was true of some. Most, however, joined up to secure a regular wage and food, and a roof over their heads. Some others, even, took the king's shilling to escape the king's justice. What united them all, though, was a feeling of superiority over foreigners, which foreign service overseas gave them an opportunity to demonstrate. It was this chauvinism, based as it was on an almost complete ignorance of the merits of other peoples and cultures, that contributed to British 'fighting spirit' in battle. In 1801 an essay by Doctor Samuel Johnson on 'The English Common Soldiers' explained the success of British arms in this way: 'Our nation may boast, beyond any other people in the world, of a kind of epidemic bravery, diffused equally through all its ranks.' Johnson warned his readers not to complain too much about the behaviour of rowdy soldiers in peacetime. As he pointed out, 'They who complain in peace of the insolence of the populace, must remember, that their insolence in peace is bravery in war.' It was not easy for Britain's allies to achieve an understanding with their British counterparts. As one allied soldier wrote: 'The English are admired as a free, an enlightened, and a brave people, but they cannot make themselves beloved; they are not content with being great, they must be thought so, and told so. They will not bend with good humour to the customs of other nations, nor will they condescend to soothe the harmless self-love of friendly foreigners. No: wherever they march or travel, they bear with them a haughty air of conscious superiority, and expect that their customs, habits and opinions should supersede, or at least suspend, those of all the countries through which they pass.' In essence, however lowly his origin, the British soldier was a snob. His sense of 'conscious superiority' sustained him in combat with his enemies and his courage was a pride in race. He regarded his military traditions as more significant than those of foreigners and his victories more momentous.

The British soldier, villain and saint as he could be, showed the best of himself at the terrible battle of Albuera. With his commander, Marshal Beresford, frankly out of his depth, his allies uncertain and his enemy overwhelming in strength and confidence, he held his ground and fought the French to a standstill before, with a final charge, he sent them fleeing in precipitate rout. Albuera is rightly famous in the regimental histories of many British units, and has served to give inspiration to generations of young soldiers who must have wondered whether they could ever match the efforts of 'that astonishing infantry'.

On 12 May 1811, General Beresford, Marshal of Portugal, was besieging the Spanish city of Badajoz, heavily fortified by the French, when he received news that a French army of 25,000 men under Marshal Soult was advancing to its relief. Abandoning the siege, Beresford pulled away to the south-east to the small town of Albuera, where he took up a defensive position. Three days later he received 14,000 Spanish reinforcements under the command of the

Spanish generals Blake and Castanos, who agreed to serve under Beresford's command. The British general now had an army of about 37,000, though many of these were Portuguese, and the newly-arrived Spanish troops were of questionable quality. Expecting the French to come from the east, Beresford made Albuera the centre of his position. Unaware that Beresford had received reinforcements, Soult attacked Beresford's position on 16 May at dawn. The French made a feint attack on the centre of the British line in the hope that Beresford would reinforce it, which in fact he did, by transferring troops from his reserve.

Meanwhile, the Spanish troops to the south of Albuera had just witnessed one of the most astonishing sights of the whole Napoleonic period (and certainly the strongest attacking force of the Peninsular War) in the shape of a massive column of 14,000 infantry, supported by artillery, and 3,500 cavalry intent on turning the left flank of the allied position. The French column was 400 yards across and 600 yards deep. Its momentum should have been irresistible. The Spanish refused to face such an onslaught and many of them fled, though others showed great gallantry in a losing cause. To support the hard-pressed Spaniards, Beresford ordered the British 2nd Division to advance and form a second line behind them. Instead of obeying orders, the division's impetuous commander General William Stewart ignored them and attacked the French without a second thought. His leading brigade of 1,600 men (Colbourne's) attacked the left flank of the huge French column, mowing down hundreds of the French with their first volley. Temporarily, Soult's column was checked. Then fate intervened. A sudden rainstorm saturated the battlefield, rendering muskets on both sides useless. Coinciding with this blow, the French cavalry (Second Hussars and Polish Second Vistula Lancers) now advanced and overran Colbourne's men, who had no protection against horsemen. Soult's Polish lancers had a field day, killing hundreds of helpless British footsoldiers with sword and lance. Within five minutes 1,300 out of 1,600 of Colbourne's men were lost, as well as five regimental colours. Some of the cavalry even tried to capture the British commander himself. But Beresford (a huge man) simply seized one Pole's lance, picking the rider out of his saddle and throwing him to the ground.

Now Hoghton's brigade appeared on the scene, followed by Abercromby's, and they formed line against the French column. Seven British battalions – about 3,700 men, two deep – faced two French divisions of about 7,800 men in column in one of the most extraordinary firefights at close range in all history. In places muskets were touching each other, and the combatants were rarely more than twenty yards apart. Volley after volley was fired, but the British 'line' held, even though Hoghton himself was killed, along with three battalion commanders. It was at this moment that Colonel Ingis of the 57th called on his men to 'Die Hard!' The British losses were dreadful: the 29th lost 336 out of 476; the 57th lost 428 out of 616; and the 48th lost 280 out of 646. French losses were never computed, though they must have been at least as heavy.

At this moment, when the strongest lead was needed from the commanders, both Beresford and Soult lost their nerve. Soult had just realized that the British had been reinforced and that he was outnumbered; he therefore went onto the defensive. Beresford, baffled by the murderous impasse between the rival infantry, had matters taken out of his hands by one of his subordinates. Fortunately, with his commander temporarily frozen with indecision, the deputy quartermaster-general, Major Henry Hardinge, took the initiative, calling up Sir Lowry Cole, commander of the 4th Division, to break the deadlock and save the British infantry, who were heavily outnumbered and would soon have been overrun. Cole brought forward 4,000 fresh infantrymen 'in line', with a protective square at each end to resist the French cavalry, if they tried to turn his flanks. The 4th Division was welcomed by a torrent of French artillery fire as well as a charge by French dragoons trying to turn their flank. Next three French columns, supported by artillery, tried to break Cole's line. Outnumbered by three to one as he was, Cole was still able to concentrate more firepower than the French, as the British line formation enabled 2,000 British troops to fire at one moment against just 360 of the French, namely those at the head of their columns. The Fusilier Brigade, consisting of the 1st and 2nd Battalions of the 7th Regiment and the 1st Battalion of the 23rd, stood their ground and fought the most bitter fight in all British military annals. Sixteen-year-old Ensign Thomas was heard to yell, 'Only with my life!' as a swarm of French cavalry tried to seize the colours of the Buffs. Thomas was killed and the colour standard taken but Lieutenant Matthew Latham leapt forward and wrestled back the colour from the French cavalryman who had it. Latham was hacked down by the Hussars, but in falling he ripped the regimental colour from its staff and bundled it into his tunic before passing out. Latham recovered, though he had lost an arm and much of his jaw in the fracas. He had saved the colour and his efforts are forever remembered in the form of a silver replica of the incident which adorns the regimental dining table.

The historian Napier relates the stirring efforts of the British infantry in this memorable account: 'The Fusilier battalions, struck by an iron tempest, reeled and staggered like sinking ships; but suddenly and sternly recovering, they closed on their terrible enemies, and then was seen with what strength and majesty the British soldier fights . . . Nothing could stop that astonishing infantry . . . The rain flowed after in streams discoloured with blood and fifteen hundred unwounded men, the remnants of 6,000 unconquerable British soldiers, stood triumphant on that fatal hill!'

There were no orders given, except 'Close in! Close up! Fire away!' Bit by bit the French were pushed back. At last the French broke and a rout began. But the victory had been dearly bought. Never before or since had British soldiers fought so bravely. In places their bodies lay three deep. The 2nd Battalion of the 7th Regiment had just 85 men left standing at the end out of 568! Sergeant Cooper of the 2nd battalion recounts what happened: 'Men are knocked about like skittles; but not a step backwards is taken. Here our colonel, Sir William Myers, and all the field officers of the brigade fall killed or wounded, but no confusion ensued . . . We are close to the enemy's columns; they break and rush down the other side of the hill in the greatest mob-like confusion.'

Beresford was too baffled by his victory to do any more than occupy the battlefield. He was very gloomy and wrote mournfully to Wellington to tell him about the battle. Losses among his Spanish and Portuguese troops had been minimal, but his British infantry had lost 4,407 out of 8,800, losses that could not be easily made good. Wellington, shocked as he was, decided that the 'victory' needed to be written up, otherwise the politicians and the public in Britain would be demanding his head. 'This won't do', he said, 'it will drive the people in England mad. Write me down a victory.' A few days later when he visited the battlefield he saw the many British dead, lying in their ranks. He also visited the wounded, telling them, 'Men of the 29th, I am sorry to see so many of you here.' One veteran sergeant replied, 'If you had commanded us, my lord, there would not be so many of us here.' But Wellington was realistic. 'Another such battle,' he commented, 'would ruin us.'

19

The Battle of Salamanca
1812

While Napoleon remained the master of Europe in 1812, Wellington's British troops in Spain comprised the irritation he could never remove. Acknowledged as a master of defensive warfare, Wellington was held in high regard by Napoleon's marshals, most of whom had tasted defeat at his hands. However, men like Soult and Marmont felt at least they had the certainty that in the French soldier they had the better marcher, even if the British soldier in action proved the steadier fighter. As a result, they believed they could always outmanoeuvre Wellington and avoid battle with him. Their men were expert foragers and had no need to placate the Spanish villagers when it came to obtaining food. The British always had to pay and remember that the Spanish were their allies. As a result of such attitudes the French tended to underestimate Wellington as a danger, fearing him only when he provoked them into attacking a position he had had time to choose, and this led directly to the battle of Salamanca, one of Wellington's greatest victories.

By the beginning of 1812 Wellington believed the strategic situation in Spain had turned in his favour. With Napoleon preparing France for its decisive campaign in Russia, the British commander was convinced that the time had come to strike a decisive blow in Spain. French forces there were split between a number of separate commands and it fell to Wellington to decide where to strike and when. Although he might have preferred to defeat Soult and free southern Spain, he decided that there was greater need to prevent Marmont from ravaging central Portugal from his base at Salamanca. For the first time Wellington would actually have equal numbers with Marmont, about 50,000 British and Portuguese troops, and this would surely be enough to ensure a decisive victory. Even the British redcoats felt confident, as Captain Kincaid of the 95th Rifles shows: 'Hitherto we had been fighting the description of battle in which John Bull glories so much – gaining a brilliant and useless victory against great odds. But we are now about to contend for fame on equal terms.'

Yet all did not go well for the British and by 21 July when Wellington moved south through Salamanca to take up a defensive position on the San Cristóbal heights he had been run ragged by Marmont's fast-marching troops and he was convinced that he had lost his chance of a decisive victory. All he sought now was to save his army by withdrawing to Ciudad Rodrigo. Marmont, certain that he had virtually trapped the British commander, now tried to sever Wellington's escape route. He based most of his manoeuvres on the unshakable belief that Wellington would never attack him but would wait to be attacked. This persuaded him that he was safe to take risks.

On the morning of 22 July, Marmont was on a hillside at Calvarrasa de Arriba. He was watching a large cloud of dust which he was certain contained the bulk of the British army retreating towards the Ciudad Rodrigo road. He believed that the British 7th division, which was opposite him, must comprise the rearguard of a retreating army. Now was the time to attack Wellington, while he was on the run. But Marmont was wrong. Wellington's army – at least most of it – was not on the move but was close to him, hidden by the high ground. The cloud of dust was being created by Packenham's 3rd division which was coming up fast from the direction of Salamanca. Marmont had fooled himself and was about to pay a high price. Unaware of how close the British were, Marmont ordered 14,000 of his men in three divisions to march westwards and pursue the dust cloud.

Wellington was having lunch and nibbling a chicken leg when news arrived that the French divisions were marching west. At first he did not believe it. 'The Devil they are!' he remarked, 'Give me my glass quickly.' From a nearby hill he scanned the French columns rushing past below him. 'By God!' he said, 'That will do!' He reputedly threw the chicken leg over his shoulder and muttered,

'*Marmont est perdu,*' before riding off to instruct his divisional commanders.

Unaware that they were each in turn exposing their flanks to the hidden British troops, the three leading French divisional commanders were rushing to destruction. First Packenham with the 3rd division arrived in time to crush the French division of General Thomière, which was in the vanguard. Minutes later the British 5th division virtually ambushed the next French troops in line, the division of General Maucune. British dragoons under Le Marchant hit Brennier's division, which never had time to form squares to resist the heavy cavalry. Wellington was ecstatic, remarking to his cavalry commander, 'By God, Cotton, I never saw anything so beautiful in my life; the day is yours.'

Almost a quarter of Marmont's army had been wiped out before the battle was half an hour old. To make matters worse for the French, Marmont was badly wounded by shrapnel and carried from the field. His replacement Bonet was killed and command fell on Bertrand Clauzel, who conducted a skilful retreat, trying to save as much of the army as he could. Many French soldiers escaped over the bridge at Alba de Tormes, which was supposed to have been held by Spanish troops under General España. Unfortunately, he had played the coward and fled to a nearby fortress with all his troops. Wellington was furious. His chance of eliminating Marmont as a potent threat had been lost by this single action. Nevertheless, he had achieved his biggest victory so far, after which there was never any further doubt as to who was the master in Spain. French generals even elevated Wellington to a rank hardly inferior to Marlborough in the pantheon of great commanders. The French suffered more than 14,000 casualties at Salamanca compared with Anglo-Portuguese losses of 5,000. Admittedly, Marmont had blundered and left himself open to attack, but who but Wellington would have reacted so quickly and so decisively? The name of Napoleon would be on everyone's lips but this master was only just beginning the campaign that would mark the turn of the tide in Europe – the march to Moscow. As he did so the 'Spanish Ulcer' was about to burst as Wellington advanced into France.

20

The Battle of Waterloo 1815

The news that Napoleon had escaped from Elba in 1814 was like an earthquake to Europe's politicians and diplomats meeting at Vienna. His return to Paris in triumph and the fact that Marshal Ney, sent by the restored Bourbons to arrest him, immediately changed sides and joined his former master showed that only a total military defeat could end the Corsican's career once and for all. But of the numerous allied generals and their massed armies, was there one who was capable of administering the *coup de grâce* to such an opponent? The campaign of the 'hundred days' began with a large question mark. Only Wellington, of all the allied generals, had yet to suffer defeat at Napoleon's hands. Could he succeed where everyone so far had failed?

By the end of May Napoleon had raised France's military strength to 284,000 men, and had an effective army of 124,500 on the Belgian border. The Allies responded quickly, raising armies of Austrians and Russians that looked impressive on paper but might not materialize for some time. The task of containing Napoleon fell to Blücher's 115,000 Prussians and Wellington's 93,000, strong Anglo-Dutch forces. Napoleon crossed into Belgium and struck first in the direction of Brussels on 15 June, but the following day his left wing under Ney was held up by Wellington at Quatre Bras. Meanwhile, on the same day, Napoleon defeated the Prussians under Marshal Blücher at Ligny, sending Marshal Grouchy's corps to pursue them and prevent them joining with Wellington, who had taken up a new position at Waterloo.

The battlefield at Waterloo had been carefully chosen by Wellington as suitable for the sort of defensive battle at which he was a master. It was very small, stretching for no more than three miles from Hougoumont in the west to the town of Papelotte in the east. The Allied and French armies took up positions on two opposing ridges, separated by a mere 1,300 yards, and into this cauldron of little more than three square miles 140,000 men and 400 guns would soon be pitched. It was a killing ground *par excellence* and offered Napoleon few opportunities for the kind of manoeuvring at which he excelled. He would be faced with few options but to assault Wellington's strong position head-on.

As the French deployed on 18 June, General d'Erlon's powerful corps of four divisions – 20,000 men – took up a position on the right, while to his left was General Reille's corps of three divisions, and behind him the mass of French cavalry under Kellermann. Further back was Lobau's VI Corps of 10,000 men, as well as more cavalry and the Imperial Guard. In total the French fielded 48,950 infantry, 15,765 cavalry, and 7,232 gunners with 246 guns.

Wellington's dispositions were based on the assumption that Blücher would come to his aid sometime during the battle and would reinforce his left wing. As a result, he had concentrated his own strength on the right wing and in the centre. As was his usual habit, he had drawn up his troops on the reverse slopes of the ridge to reduce casualties from the French artillery. The right of the Allied line between Merbraine and the Nivelle road was held by 'Daddy' Hill's II Corps, while to his left was the Prince of Orange's I Corps and Sir Thomas Picton's reserve division. The extreme left of the Allied line was held by Prince Bernard of Saxe-Weimar with the cavalry brigades of Vandaleur and Vivian. In support of the centre was Lord Uxbridge's cavalry. Wellington had also occupied several advanced positions to act as breakers to the waves of French attacks, the most important of which was the château of Hougoumont, held by Nassauers, Hanoverians and units of the Coldstream Guards. Another was the farmhouse of La Haie Sainte, held by men of the King's German Legion. In total Wellington's force comprised 49,608 infantry, 12,408 cavalry, and 5,645 gunners with 156 artillery pieces, being made up of 13,253 British, 6,387 King's German Legion, 15,935 Hanoverians, 29,214 Dutch and Belgians, 6,808 Brunswickers and 2,880 Nassauers.

Such were the troops who were actually on the battlefield. But just as important were the ones who were not present, like Grouchy's corps of 30,000 men which was supposed to be pursuing the Prussians from Ligny and yet failed both to keep Blücher from reaching Waterloo and to reach the battlefield itself. Much of the fault for this rested with Napoleon himself, whose messages to Grouchy were unclear and failed to entertain the possibility that the Prussians might evade the marshal and return to help Wellington. When Soult had suggested recalling Grouchy without delay before the battle of Waterloo began, Napoleon had pooh-poohed the idea. And when it was suggested that Blücher was planning to come to Wellington's aid, which explained the weak Allied left wing, Napoleon exploded with anger. He was working to his preconceptions, and this time he was wrong.

At Waterloo Napoleon was far from well and was suffering from the piles that plagued him in his later years. He was short-tempered and snappy and, worst of all, contemptuous of his enemy. Wellington was a bad general, or so Napoleon claimed, and his army would be driven off its ridge by massive frontal assaults. When Soult reminded him of Wellington's record in Spain it only seemed to make the emperor more determined to break him by main force.

The rain of the previous few days had made the terrain heavy and difficult for both infantry and cavalry assaults, and so Napoleon decided to delay his attack until as late as possible to allow the ground to dry. But every minute wasted added to the danger that the Prussians would come to Wellington's assistance. An attack by mid-morning might have stretched the Iron Duke too far and made his defeat by mid-afternoon inevitable. However, unknown to Napoleon, Marshal Blücher – a battle-scarred veteran, who veered between fits of drunkenness and senile melancholia – had detached Bülow's I Corps with instructions to make all possible haste to reach Waterloo, and the Prussian II Corps was following. In a message to Wellington, received early on the morning of the battle, Blücher had written, 'Say in my name to the Duke of Wellington that, ill as I am, I will march at the head of my army to attack without delay the right flank of the enemy, if Napoleon should attempt anything against the Duke.' With Gneisenau watching Grouchy, 'Old Forwards' Blücher rode through the muddy, sunken roads of Belgium to join Bülow, shouting to his men as he passed, 'Lads, you will not let me break my word!'

Prince Jerome Bonaparte's division began the battle with a diversionary attack on the château of Hougoumont, hoping to persuade Wellington to thin his centre to support the position. But Jerome's stupidity was to have entirely the reverse effect. Sensitive to his own modest military record when compared with that of his brother, he wanted very much to capture Hougoumont at whatever the cost and mulishly besieged the château and its outbuildings as if the fate of the whole empire depended on his success. The Allied defenders fought from within the buildings, firing through prepared loopholes, taking a steady toll of the French attackers. Soon Jerome had to call up help from General Foy's division, and as the vicious struggle in and around the château escalated it soon involved most of General Reille's II Corps, weakening the whole French left centre. To support Hougoumont cost Wellington just 13 companies of the Coldstream Guards, while it robbed Napoleon of a quarter of his infantry. On a day of swaying fortunes the Allies held Hougoumont by prodigies of valour throughout the battle. In 1818 an English clergyman decided to confer a small annuity on a British soldier who had shown great courage at the battle of Waterloo. The Duke of Wellington was asked to choose a worthy recipient for the award and handed on the difficult task to Sir John Byng. Byng decided to make his choice from the 2nd Brigade of Guards, which had distinguished itself in the defence of Hougoumont. There were many gallant candidates, but the choice finally fell on Sergeant James Graham, of the light company of the Coldstream Guards.

The defence of the château of Hougoumont was one of the decisive moments of the entire battle. Had the French been able to take it, they would have been able to turn Wellington's position on the ridge. Napoleon, however, had underestimated the fighting quality of the British Guards, who defended the château. Despite being heavily outnumbered and with the buildings burning all around them, they clung on grimly throughout a whole day of the fiercest fighting. At one point a huge French officer, Lieutenant Legros, nicknamed *L'Enfonceur*, (the Smasher) broke his way through the great north door and, followed by a handful of wildly cheering men, rushed into the courtyard. Facing him was Sergeant James Graham, also a giant among men. Of the Frenchmen who had followed Legros most were killed on the spot; and, as the few survivors ran back, five of the Guards – Colonel Macdonnell, Captain Wyndham, Ensign Gooch, Ensign Hervey and Sergeant Graham – by sheer strength, closed the gate again, in spite of the efforts of the French from outside, and effectually barricaded it against further assaults. Over and through the loopholed wall of the courtyard, the English garrison now kept up a deadly fire of musketry, which was fiercely answered by the French, who swarmed round the curtilage. Shells from their batteries were falling fast into the besieged place, one of which set part of the mansion and some of the outbuildings on fire. Graham, who was at this time standing near Colonel Macdonell at the wall, and who had shown the most perfect steadiness and courage, now asked permission of his commanding officer to retire for a moment. Macdonell replied, 'By all means, Graham; but I wonder you should ask leave now.' Graham answered, 'I would not, sir, only my brother is wounded and he is in that outbuilding there, which has just caught fire.' Laying down his musket, Graham ran to the blazing spot, lifted up his brother, and laid him in a ditch. Then he was back at his post, and was plying his musket against the French again before his absence was noticed, except by his colonel.

Meanwhile, Napoleon had drawn up 84 guns to support d'Erlon's attempt to drive a hole straight through Wellington's centre. But he soon found that the wet ground simply absorbed the heavy shot, muffling explosions and preventing the solid shot ricocheting. In addition, Wellington's tactic of positioning his men on the reverse slope meant that they suffered few casualties from the French barrage. At 1.00 p.m. d'Erlon's massive corps was ready to go, but Napoleon now received reports that troops were unexpectedly appearing from the northeast – not Grouchy's men but the advance guard of Bülow's corps of 30,000 men. Napoleon at last wrote a peremptory order to Grouchy to march to Waterloo – but it was too late now and only reached the marshal at 5.00 p.m. For Napoleon there was no time to waste; Wellington must be driven off his ridge without delay.

Sending part of Lobau's infantry and cavalry units under Domont and Subservie to hold the right flank against von Bülow, at 1.30 p.m. Napoleon ordered d'Erlon's corps to advance across the valley towards the Allies on the ridge. But at the start a terrible mistake was made. Instead of advancing in battalion columns – presenting a narrow front – d'Erlon's men advanced in massive division columns, 200 men wide and with a depth of 24–27 men, offering the British gunners unmissable targets. The French casualties were truly shocking as they crossed the 1,300 yards separating them from the Allies on the ridge. To make matters worse, d'Erlon's men were advancing without adequate artillery or cavalry cover. On the ridge the British guns had been set up behind a strong hedge and fired with impunity through holes hacked in the thicket. As d'Erlon's depleted columns reached the top of the slope they were met by Picton's 3,000 British redcoats, who fired a volley with their old 'Brown Bess' muskets and charged into them at the point of the bayonet. It was the first crisis of the battle and, though Picton was killed – shot through his top hat – his men swept the French back. D'Erlon's corps was simultaneously hit by two of Lord Uxbridge's heavy cavalry brigades: Somerset's Household Brigade of Life Guards, Dragoon Guards and Horse Guards, and Ponsonby's Union Brigade of Royal Scots Greys, Blues and Royals and Iniskillings. Three thousand of d'Erlon's men were taken prisoner at this time and the rest were driven back across the valley. Napoleon's sledgehammer attack had failed completely. However, the over-excited cavalry of Ponsonby's Union Brigade, having defeated d'Erlon, then charged the French guns, only to be counterattacked by Napoleon's lancers and cuirassiers: over 1,000 of Uxbridge's 2,500 British cavalry were lost in this moment of madness, including Ponsonby, killed by a French lancer.

By 3.00 p.m. Napoleon knew that he could expect no help from Grouchy. To continue the battle meant increasing numbers of Prussians would join the Allied left wing until the French were overwhelmed by weight of numbers. Yet he refused to withdraw, telling Marshal Ney that the position at La Haie Sainte would have to be taken at whatever the cost. Ney led an assault on the ridge, during which he noticed Allied troops retreating – they were probably ambulance workers or men collecting ammunition – but Ney got it into his head that Wellington's army was on the point of breaking up. There now occurred one of the most extraordinary and yet majestic incidents in Napoleonic warfare, commemorated in dozens of paintings since 1815. Without infantry or artillery support, Ney called up 5,000 French cavalry to assault the ridge in what he believed would be a decisive attack. The British responded by forming squares to receive the cavalry – in fact twenty large rectangles would be a better description – and the tide of French horsemen simply washed over these 'rocks' without doing much harm. The Allied gunners stayed outside the squares until the last possible moment in order to fire their pieces with shattering effect into the masses of men and horses riding towards them. The French cavalry rode over the British guns, but apparently did not think to disable them. Once the French retreated the gunners emerged from the squares and began firing again. It had been a magnificently picturesque but ultimately pointless exercise. Napoleon, viewing the destruction of his cavalry from a distance, was infuriated at Ney's stupidity. Meanwhile, by 4.00 p.m. the Prussians were emerging from the woods on the French right and engaging Napoleon's covering troops. Time was running out. A second – and even larger – cavalry assault, 10,000-strong, on the British squares was at that moment being defeated around La Haie Sainte. But at this – France's most desperate moment – Ney recovered his nerve and organized a coordinated attack on the strategic farmhouse, with artillery cover for an infantry and cavalry assault, and succeeded in driving the King's German Legion from the buildings they had held since early morning. Bringing up a battery of guns, Ney now began to smash the British squares with artillery fire. This was the greatest crisis of the day. The exhausted Allied troops on the ridge really were on the point of breaking this time, and Ney sent urgent gallopers calling Napoleon to send up more troops. But Napoleon was beside himself with rage at the way Ney had squandered his cavalry, and refused to release the Imperial Guard, replying to Ney's urgent call with the scornful words, 'Troops! Where does he expect me to get them from? Make them?'

If Napoleon was missing his chance of victory by not supporting Ney, Wellington was nevertheless aware that the marshal's men had to be silenced at all costs. Taking personal command of a brigade of Brunswickers, he rode across to plug the hole that Ney had smashed in his line. He need not have worried, for more and more Prussians were reaching the field now, including Pirch's II

Corps and Zieten's I Corps, which rode round to support the Allied left on the ridge. It was too late for Napoleon to do anything more than extricate his army before it was destroyed. But he refused to concede the battle. Believing that his Imperial Guard could still break Wellington's hold on the ridge, he ordered his officers to tell their men that the troops arriving on their right were Grouchy's and not Prussians – a lie that was soon discovered and caused morale to collapse. Nevertheless, the Imperial Guard advanced with measured tread to the sound of the drums, according to Benjamin Haydon they were 'tall bony men with black moustachios, gigantic caps, depravity, indifference and bloodthirstiness burnt in their faces; more dreadful-looking men I had never seen'. As they marched up the slopes Wellington ordered his men to lie down so that the shot from the French artillery flew harmlessly over their heads. When the magnificent veterans of earlier Napoleonic battles reached the top of the ridge 'with high, hairy caps and long red feathers nodding to the beat of the drum', they were hit at short range by a fusillade of musket fire and grape shot. At Wellington's order, the British Guards leapt to their feet and at just twenty yards' range fired a volley into the French ranks, then charged them with the bayonet. Whether Wellington really said, 'Up Guards and at 'em,' is less important than the fact that Maitland's Guards brigade did exactly that. To the French soldier the Imperial Guard represented all that was best in his army and his nation. Yet, incredibly, the guardsmen were being driven back all along the line. The cry went up, '*La Garde recule!*' and the news spread like wildfire. Sensing the moment had come to attack, Wellington, mounted on his grey, 'Copenhagen', raised his hat and ordered a general advance. From the ridge to which they had been pinned all day, the whole Allied line moved forward. It was too much for the Imperial Guards and many raised the cry of beaten French troops throughout history: '*Sauve qui peut!*'

Napoleon's army was disintegrating and the emperor was persuaded to leave the stricken field to try to rally the survivors at Genappe. Many famous regiments had lost all cohesion and become mobs of terrified and beaten men. Still on the battlefield, General Cambronne showed great courage when called upon to surrender the Guard. He is quoted as replying, 'The Guard dies but never surrenders,' but some claim he merely shouted *'Merde!'* Meanwhile, as it grew dark, Blücher and Wellington met at La Belle Alliance, the old Prussian grasping Wellington's hand with the words, *'Mein lieber Kamerad! Quelle affaire.'* Under Gneisenau's directions the Prussians took up the pursuit of the remnants of Napoleon's Armée du Nord.

The casualties in this memorable but savage encounter had been heavy on both sides. Out of a total force of 72,000 the French had lost 41,000 men killed, wounded or taken prisoner – 57 per cent, the highest percentage losses ever suffered in a Napoleonic battle – as well as 220 guns. Wellington's army had lost 15,100 and the Prussians 7,000 – more than in many a defeat. In every sense Waterloo had been a fight to the finish. No one had much stomach for any further campaigning after this bloodbath. Wellington had been shocked by his experience: 'In all my life I have not experienced such anxiety, for I must confess I have never been so close before to defeat.'

21

The Battle of Balaclava 1854

The Crimean War threw up its fair share of notable characters and contained vivid episodes that filled the newspapers of Victorian Britain. Yet even the work of 'the lady with the lamp', Florence Nightingale, could not seize the front pages from the epic story of the 'Charge of the Light Brigade'. Yet this most famous incident in British military history – possibly in all military history – occurred in a battle that was essentially little more than a skirmish and far less significant than the later struggle at Inkerman. It was the human interest of the story that was beloved of the Victorian reader, its combination of courage in the face of overwhelming danger and stupidity amongst the ruling classes. The Victorians loved to read of dashing Captain Nolan and Jemmy the terrier as much as of mistaken orders by aristocrats who should have known better.

On arrival in the Crimea in 1854, the British had established their base at the port of Balaclava and, with their French and Turkish allies, had concentrated their efforts on besieging the Russian naval base at Sebastapol. The Russian field commander in the Crimea, Prince Menshikov, received direct orders from St. Petersburg to relieve pressure on Sebastapol by attacking Balaclava on 25 October. The British resisted in inimitable style, turning defeat into victory and setbacks into triumphs, and bringing to the science of warfare the clumsy antics of the public schoolboy. The 93rd Highlanders created one legend, that of 'the thin red line tipped with steel'. The Heavy Brigade made one of the greatest and most effective cavalry charges of the nineteenth century, which was immediately forgotten. The Light Brigade made one of the most ill-advised charges in all military history and was remembered evermore. It was a curious battle.

It was early morning on 25 October when the Russian cavalry took the sleepy British commanders completely by surprise by overrunning the Allied defenders on Canrobert Hill and threatening to attack the British base at Balaclava. All that stood in their way was Sir Colin Campbell with the 93rd Highlanders, about to enter British military history as 'the thin red line'. The 93rd, just 550 Highland soldiers, covered a front of about 150 yards. Under constant fire from Russian artillery, they faced a mass of Russian Hussars bearing down on them. Alongside them Turkish troops had panicked and fled into the British camp in disorder, attacked as they passed by one of the Scotsmen's brawny wives with a broom. Mrs Fanny Duberly, riding up to see what was going on, encountered the flying Turks. As she commented, 'Had I known of their brutal cowardice I should have ridden over them all.'

As the Russian cavalry bore down on the line of Highlanders they were astonished to find that the 93rd did not form up the 'square', the traditional defence of infantry against cavalry. Instead they stood their ground in just two lines, bringing all their muskets into play simultaneously. As they waited, Campbell's voice could be heard: 'There's no retreat from here, men! You must die where you stand.' Again group solidarity was the answer. The men of the 93rd would live and fight and die together. Private John Scott replied to Campbell, 'Aye, aye, Sir Colin, and needs be we'll do that.' As their Turkish allies fled some of the Scotsmen began to grow restive, as if they wanted to charge the Russians rather than wait to receive them. But Campbell was up to his task, one of the few British officers of his day who really was, and snapped at them: '93rd! 93rd! Damn all that eagerness!' As the Russian Hussars broke into a canter and then a charge, the 93rd fired a first volley and then calmly reloaded. A second calm volley at 250 yards brought many riders tumbling down. And now the Hussars began to sheer away from their indomitable opponents. But the 93rd were not finished with them. As they rode towards the right flank of the line the Grenadier Company of the 93rd hit them with a third shattering volley that sent them racing away in disorder. The British camp was saved as the Highlanders tossed their feathered hats into the air.

By this time the cavalry commander, Lord Lucan, had ridden up to the commander of the Heavy Brigade and ordered General Scarlett to charge the Russian cavalry. Scarlett needed no second invitation and the first line of Greys and Iniskillings smashed into the Russian horse, supported from behind by the second and third lines of Dragoon Guards and Royals. Soon an epic cavalry battle was taking place. Within eight minutes the Russians were routed and fleeing.

It was at this stage that matters took a different turn. The Russians had set up a strong artillery battery of Don Cossacks at the end of the North Valley. In addition, the Odessky Regiment had been sent to occupy the redoubts recently vacated by the Turks and, in doing so, to capture the British guns abandoned at the beginning of the battle. Lord Raglan had few troops available to prevent this. The infantry was not yet in a position to intervene and so he had to rely on the Light Brigade which, so far, had not been involved in the fighting. Lord Raglan decided to order his cavalry to regain the redoubts and the guns, and operate with the infantry that should soon be arriving. He therefore sent instructions to Lord Lucan. The disparity between what the British commander-in-chief meant in his message to Lord Lucan and what Lucan understood by it was partly a reflection of the confusion in the minds of the men involved. It was also a product of the different positions they had taken up and their dissimilar fields of vision. The first message read, 'Cavalry to advance and take advantage of any opportunity to recover the Heights. They will be supported by the infantry, which have been ordered to advance on two fronts.' Lucan was uneasy on receiving this note and did nothing for 45 minutes. Did Raglan mean that he should wait for the infantry to arrive before he did anything? If so, where were the infantry?

From his vantage point Lord Raglan could see that his orders were not being followed. General Scarlett's Heavy Brigade had thrown the enemy into disorder. Why had the Light Brigade not reinforced that charge and swept the Russians from their redoubts? What on earth was Lucan doing just sitting waiting? This was too much for Lord Raglan who dictated another order to General Airey, who scribbled the words on a piece of paper before giving it to an ADC, Captain Nolan. It is doubtful if this message was any clearer than the last one. 'Lord Raglan wishes the cavalry to advance rapidly to the front – follow the enemy and try to prevent the enemy carrying away the guns. Troop Horse Artillery may accompany. French cavalry is on your left. Immediate. Airey.'

Captain Nolan, renowned rider and hothead, spurred his horse down the hill. As he departed he heard Raglan's final words to him, 'Tell Lord Lucan the cavalry is to attack immediately.' Nolan replied, 'I'll lead them myself. I'll lead them on.' But Lucan was still unsure, even when Nolan insisted he should attack at once. What was he supposed to attack? At ground level the situation was less clear to him than it was to Raglan on the heights. What guns was Raglan referring to? At this Nolan gestured furiously, 'There is your enemy! There are your guns!' But Lucan still could not see any Russians towing away guns. Why he did not send anyone to a high point to identify his targets is inexplicable and it was this failure that was to lead directly to disaster. The only guns he could actually see were sited at the far end of the North Valley. He assumed, therefore, that these were the guns that Raglan meant. Pointing down the valley towards the Russian guns, Lucan ordered Lord Cardigan to lead the Light Brigade to the attack. Both Lucan and Cardigan knew that it was a suicidal order but felt they had no alternative but to obey. They were being asked to capture guns more than a mile and a half away, all the time riding down a valley controlled by Russian cavalry and massed infantry, firing at them from the heights on both sides. It was truly 'the valley of death'. Yet those were the orders as far as they could see. So, resplendent in gold braid at the head of his 'cherry bums', Lord Cardigan led forward his brigade of 673 men. Nolan had insisted on accompanying the Light Brigade and at once took the lead, riding ahead of Cardigan to his lordship's fury. In fact, Nolan was in the process of crossing from left to right, probably realizing that Cardigan was heading the wrong way, when he was hit in the chest and killed by shell splinters. General Bosquet, watching from the heights, muttered his immortal words *'C'est magnifique mais ce n'est pas la guerre'*, which the British have proudly assumed was a compliment, omitting the second part of the Frenchman's observation, which sets the whole in perspective – *'C'est de la folie.'* Fortunately, Bosquet did not rest on his laurels and confine his assistance to the merely verbal kind. Instead, he called up the 4th *Chasseurs d'Afrique* to cover those of the Light Brigade who might survive the charge. From his vantage point Raglan concluded that, 'Cardigan had lost his head.' The Russians simply assumed that these madmen charging towards their guns were drunk. Afterwards, General Liprandi questioned one prisoner as to what his officers had given him to make him charge like that. The trooper replied, 'By God, if we had so much as smelt the barrel we would have taken half Russia by this time.'

There were post mortems in abundance. Raglan's verdict was clear from his remark to Lucan, 'You have lost the Light Brigade!' Perhaps he was right, but in the heat of battle there is little time for interpreting an apparently baffling order from a commander. A subordinate officer must simply obey the order he believes he has been given. Most accounts of Balaclava simply end at this point as if the battle were over. Far from it. The Light Brigade had overrun the Russian guns, cutting down the gunners and then charging the Russian cavalry assembled behind their artillery. But what were they to do next? They had no orders and no commander either. Cardigan, having survived the charge by the skin of his teeth, assumed he had done all that was required of him and rode back down the valley, congratulating the wounded as he passed on his way. Fortunately, his second-in-command, Lord George Paget, took his work more seriously. He rallied the remnants of the brigade and prepared to face the hordes of Russian cavalry that now descended on the Light Brigade. It was the *Chasseurs d'Afrique* who saved the day, driving off the Russian horsemen and ensuring that the survivors of the mad charge lived to tell the tale. Paget was so disgusted at Cardigan's display that he later resigned his commission. Of the 673 men who had joined the charge, just 195 survived. The 13th Light Dragoons was reduced to two officers and eight men and more than 500 of the brigade's horses had died. Pleasant to relate, a regimental terrier named Jemmy who also entered the 'valley of death' came back, with shell splinters in his neck but otherwise hale and hearty. Jemmy survived and returned to England with his regiment. Cardigan always insisted the blame was not his. As he spoke to the wounded he told them, 'Men, it was a mad-brained trick, but it was no fault of mine!' With the adrenaline still flowing many of the survivors called out, 'Go again, my lord!'

The Russian plan to attack Balaclava had failed and so the battle ended when they withdrew into Sebastapol. It had been Campbell's and Scarlett's day – and perhaps Bosquet's – but it would be remembered more for that bunch of ninnies Raglan, Lucan and Cardigan. It had been a victory of sorts, not a glorious defeat, and should be remembered instead for the work of professionals like the 93rd Highlanders and the troopers of the Heavy Brigade.

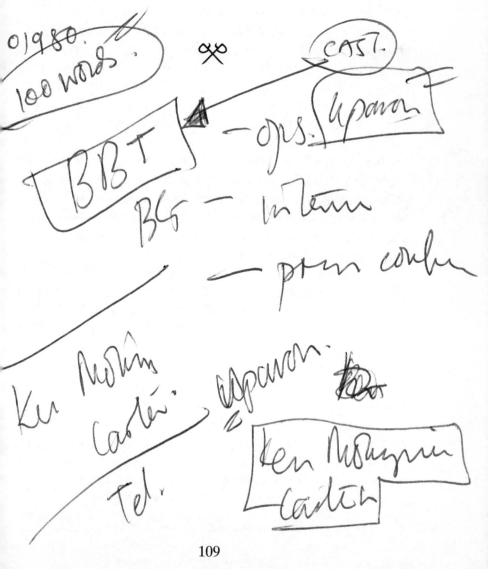

22

The Battle of Inkerman
1854

Writers who have dealt with the subject of fighting spirit have generally assumed that soldierly morale is, among other things, normally dependent on the way in which the soldier is treated. If he is neglected, badly clothed and fed, led into disaster by idiotic officers and given the impression that he counts for little, it is generally assumed that his combat performance will suffer. The British army in the Crimean War, however, provides an almost entirely contrary picture. Several times during the campaign in the Crimea, the British soldier revealed a spirit and a fortitude completely at odds with the abysmal treatment he was receiving from his own officers and administration. High morale was maintained in conditions that should have ensured discontent if not actually mutiny on the part of the common soldier.

On campaign the welfare of British soldiers was the responsibility of the Commissariat, but so deficient was this organization in the field that complaints flooded back to London, with the result that in February 1855 Sir John McNeill and Colonel Alexander Tulloch were sent out to the Crimea to report. What they found was little less than a national scandal. The Commissioners were particularly concerned about the quality and quantity of the men's diet. It was obvious that the men were often reduced to half rations at short notice and sometimes received nothing. One example they cited concerned 25 December, 1854 – Christmas Day and even on campaign a traditional day of celebration in the British army – when Colonel Bell's command received no food at all. The Colonel, quite reasonably, 'kicked up a dust' with a commissary office and eventually some small portions of fresh meat were served out, but by that time it was dark and the men had no fires or means of cooking it. Salt meat and biscuit were generally available but these gave insufficient nutritional value to men working such long hours and in such terrible conditions. Research has shown that the Crimean soldier was receiving food of less nutritional value than inmates of British prisons! Nor, although lime juice was available in great quantities aboard one of the ships in Balaclava harbour, was any of it circulated to the troops, even though many of them were succumbing to scurvy. Coffee beans were distributed to the men, but only in their raw, uncooked form. As one officer remarked, 'A ration of green raw coffee berry was served out; a mockery in the midst of all this misery. Nothing to roast coffee, nothing to grind it, no fire, no sugar; and unless it was meant that we eat it as horses do barley, I don't see what use the men could make of it, except what they have just done, pitched it into the mud.' In fact, the British soldiers were more resourceful than that. Some of them ground the coffee with cannon balls and cut their dried meat into strips to make fuel to roast the coffee beans.

As well as poor food, the British soldiers had been equipped with unsuitable clothing. The main problem was their boots, which were inadequate for the harsh conditions of a Crimean winter. In the snow men often wore two pairs of socks, while others suffered from swollen feet from long periods of duty in the soggy trenches. The British boots were so badly made that the following curious incident seems to symbolize the entire Commissariat effort in the Crimea. On 1 February 1855, the 55th Regiment paraded in 'a vast black dreary wilderness of mud'. The men sank into the slime and as they tried to march away, all the boot soles were sucked off. The men simply threw away the boots and marched off to the front in their socks! It is against this background that one needs to set the combat performance of the British army during the Crimean War. What is ironical is that the confidence of the soldier in his own ability, and in that of his regiment, was perhaps higher at this time than at any other in British history.

The battle of Inkerman has been described as one of the noblest battles ever fought by the British army. Certainly, it is probably one of the most confused battles of the nineteenth century, and as such defies description. It was a true 'soldier's battle' in which the role of the commander devolved upon subalterns as a result of the close fighting and the prevailing fog. The enemy were everywhere, it seemed, in front, behind and frequently all around the heavily outnumbered British soldiers. Even the superior fire discipline of the British and the greater hitting power of their Minié rifles were reduced by the close-range fighting. Much of the fighting, indeed, resembled more a huge mêlée in which muskets were used as clubs and men wrestled each other to the ground. Frequently outnumbered ten to one, the redcoats fought with unimaginable savagery.

The fog at Inkerman was both physical and metaphorical. While the British floundered about in the mists, unable to see either friend or foe clearly, the Russian troops were led by generals who refused to cooperate with each other and who sent them into action without orders and over terrain they had never seen before. Most of the Russian troops involved in the battle had only arrived the previous day from Bessarabia and had never even seen a map of the Crimea.

Yet the fog was vital to the British, by concealing from the Russian masses how few were their opponents. Prince Menshikov's assault troops numbered 60,000 men as well as 234 guns, against fewer than 10,000 British and French in the vicinity of Cossack Hill. Given one glimpse of the truth, the Russians would have taken heart and swept away the few redcoats who stood in their path.

The first indication that an enemy attack was taking place was when all the bells of Sebastapol began ringing and the British pickets on Shell Hill were all captured by the Tomsky Regiment, which had climbed unseen and unheard until they were within touching distance of the British sentries. The main Russian assault fell on the British 2nd Division, temporarily commanded by Brigadier-General Pennefather, an Irish officer prone to falling to blows rather than asking questions, and one splendidly fitted to a battle like Inkerman. When General Cathcart rode up to ask him where his 4th Division was needed, Pennefather replied, 'Everywhere'. Pennefather was right. Not so fortunate was the first French officer to offer assistance. When General Bosquet rushed two French regiments to the aid of the British he encountered two British divisional commanders, Cathcart and Sir George Brown, both survivors of Wellington's battles in Spain and both gallophobic. They politely thanked Bosquet for his offer but told him the British could manage on their own and certainly without French help. Although Bosquet withdrew temporarily he kept his regiments at the ready for when he knew they would be needed later.

One group of Coldstream Guards, lost in the fog, spotted Sir Charles Russell and called out to him, 'If any officer will lead us we will charge.' No blue-blooded British aristocrat could resist such an invitation. Russell went over to them and said, 'Come on, my lads, who will follow me?' With a cheer the guardsmen followed Russell down into the Russian masses. In the confused fighting that followed Russell suddenly felt a gentle tap on his shoulder. He turned to find Private Anthony Palmer looking at him. 'You was nearly done for', said Palmer. Apparently a Russian had been about to bayonet Russell in the back when Palmer saw the danger and killed the Russian with his rifle-butt. Another of Russell's followers, Private Bancroft, was in the heart of the struggle: 'I bayonetted the first Russian in the chest; he fell dead. I was then stabbed in the mouth with great force, which caused me to stagger back, where I shot this second Russian and shot a third through. A fourth and fifth came at me and ran me through the right side. I fell but managed to run one through and brought him down. I stunned him by kicking him, whilst I was engaging my bayonet with another. Sergeant-Major Alger called out to me not to kick the man that was down, but not being dead he was very troublesome to my legs; I was fighting the other over his body. I returned to the Battery and spat out my teeth; I found two only.'

At Sandbag Battery, a few hundred British troops, mainly guardsmen, led by Sir George Cathcart and the Duke of Cambridge were virtually surrounded by three Russian battalions. In the immortal words of Sir George, just before he was killed, 'We are in a scrape.' One sergeant called out that they needed 'the greatest miracle in the world'. Assistant-Surgeon Wolseley, returning from helping some wounded, found himself blocked by hundreds of Russian soldiers. Undeterred, he rounded up some guardsmen from near at hand. As he went on, 'I was the only officer in sight and gave the order, "Fix bayonets, charge, and keep up the hill." We charged through losing, I should think, about half our number.' This charge completely unsettled the Russians, who in the fog could not tell if it presaged an even larger assault. They fell back, allowing Cambridge and his guardsmen to wriggle out of their trap. Elsewhere, Captain Burnaby of the Grenadier Guards charged nearly seven hundred Russians with just twenty of his men and put them to flight. The French general Bosquet saw the slaughter around the Sandbag Battery after the battle and commented, '*Quel abattoir!*' The British and Russians had fought to the last man for control of this useless feature, which had changed hands a dozen times and cost hundreds of lives.

The Russians were fighting a battle that they could not win. They were fighting British history and regimental tradition. In the terrible blood-soaked encounters in the surreal atmosphere of that foggy day, they were up against regiments who counted Minden and Albuera on their list of battle-honours. And the men remembered the spirit with which those other men, those regimental heroes of yesteryear, had fought in similar impossible actions and were inspired by the knowledge that they had triumphed over the odds. From the 20th Regiment welled up the 'unearthly Minden yell' as they drove the Russian Iakoutsk Regiment at bayonet point towards a ravine. From another part of the field the officers of the 57th, the 'Diehards', enjoined their men to 'Remember Albuera!'

After perhaps eight hours of fighting the last Russian assault was turned back when French reinforcements – 2,000 Zouaves from North Africa under General Bosquet – finally came to the help of the British, who were wilting. The British commander-in-chief, Lord Raglan, who had contributed nothing to the battle so far, at least welcomed the French with a memorable smile and copious thanks. '*Au nom d'Angleterre, je vous remercie,*' he said to Bosquet. The Guards' commander, the Duke of Cambridge, who had borne a charmed life throughout the fight, had just 200 of his 1,300 elite guardsmen still standing by this time. Of the 35,000 Russians who were actively involved in the battle, more than 11,000 of them were killed or seriously wounded.

Historians have found patterns in the action at Inkerman, yet there were few that made any sense to the common soldiers. It was the reporter from *The Times*, W. H. Russell, who summed up the historical significance of the battle and of the fighting spirit of these incredible men: 'It is considered that the soldiers who met these furious columns of the Czar were the remnants of three British divisions, which scarcely numbered 8,500; that they were hungry and wet, and half-famished; that they were belonging to a force which was generally "out of bed" four nights out of seven; which had been enfeebled by sickness, by severe toil, sometimes for twenty-four hours at a time without relief of any kind; but among them were men who had within a short time previously lain out for forty-eight hours in the trenches at a stretch – it will be readily admitted that never was a more extraordinary contest maintained by our army since it acquired a reputation in the world's history.' Perhaps the last words on Inkerman should be left to General Pennefather, hero among heroes: 'I tell you, we gave 'em a hell of a towelling.'

23

The Siege of Delhi 1857

The Indian Mutiny of 1857 was the greatest shock to the British Empire in the nineteenth century. For a tense matter of months it seemed likely that the British hold on India would be broken by a general uprising against the British East India Company. The spark that ignited the revolt was the imposition on the sepoys, both Muslims and Hindus, of new cartridges greased with pork or beef fat, that challenged their religious beliefs. Mutiny flared into life when the Indian troops at Meerut, some 36 miles to the north-east of the capital city of Delhi, refused to use the greased cartridges they were given, attacked European cantonments there and then headed towards Delhi, being joined by floods of sepoys from many other British camps. The mutineers chose Delhi as the centre of the mutiny and the last Moghul emperor, Bahadur Shah II, to be their figurehead. His palace, known as the Red Fort, thus became the focal point for British reaction. Only when it had been captured could the mutiny be brought under control.

The first British troops to arrive at Delhi were 4,000 men from Ambala under General Sir Henry Bernard, and the European troops from the Meerut garrison commanded by Colonel Archdale Wilson. Outside the walls of the city they defeated the mutineer army of 30,000 men, driving them within the city walls and occupying a two-mile-long ridge 40 feet high which ran alongside the Western Jumna Canal. Unfortunately, they burned the mutineer's barracks as a reprisal and by so doing denied themselves any shelter during the heat of the Indian summer. They then settled in for one of the most astonishing sieges in all history. It is questionable if so small a force has ever besieged so large a city with so big a garrison.

While the Mutiny swept through northern India, with countless atrocities and just as many acts of heroism, the British ringed

Delhi and waited. Generals came and went, usually in coffins as a result of the heat and the cholera. Barnard died, to be replaced by Reed, who was forced by ill health to hand over to Archdale Wilson. Wilson was frankly out of his depth but he showed stubborn determination until he received two pieces of good news: first that Sir Colin Campbell, whom we saw earlier at Balaclava with his 93rd Highlanders, had sailed from Britain with reinforcements. Then came the news that everyone was waiting for – John Nicholson was coming from the Punjab with his movable column. Nicholson's forces would double the number of besiegers at a stroke but it was not numbers alone that counted. Nicholson's reputation alone was worth an army.

There is no doubt that the hero of the siege of Delhi was John Nicholson, VC, known as the 'Lion of the Punjab'. No British soldier of the nineteenth century – or possibly any other century for that matter – was held in such high esteem by everyone who knew him. To list some of the opinions his contemporaries expressed about this giant of a man is to do him no more than justice.

Sir Herbert Edwards, Nicholson's colleague in the Punjab: *'A nobler spirit never went forth to fight his country's battles . . . I never saw another like him, and never expect to do so.'*

Field-Marshal Lord Roberts, victor in the Second Afghan War and commander-in-chief in the Second Boer War: *'I have never seen any one like him. He was the beau-ideal of a soldier and a gentleman.'*

Lord Dalhousie, the Governor-General of India: *'A tower of strength . . . His name cowed whole provinces while he was yet scores of miles away.'*

General Sir Hugh Gough, British commander in the Sikh Wars: *'The idol of all soldiers.'*

Sir John Lawrence, the Commissioner of the Punjab: *'Without John Nicholson Delhi could never have fallen . . . The memory of his deeds will never perish as long as British rule endures.'*

Few if any British soldiers have been deified by their enemies and have turned their fiercest opponents into their firmest allies, but that is what John Nicholson achieved. The Pathans and many of the peoples of the Punjab and Afghanistan worshipped Nicholson

(Nikal Seyn) as a god, and set up shrines to him. He was the greatest swordsman in India; on one occasion, during the siege of Delhi, he cut a sepoy in two with a single blow. Throughout the Mutiny he was like an 'avenging angel'. He recommended new punishments for mutineers, such as flaying alive, impalement or burning alive. He shot many mutineers from cannons. His hatred of the sepoy was implacable – perhaps pathological.

Born in Dublin in 1822, John Nicholson was the eldest son of a doctor, who died when he was just ten. John was brought up by a mother whom he adored then and throughout his life. With the help of his uncle, a Director of the East India Company, John joined the Bengal army in 1839 and served in the First Afghan War, being imprisoned by the Afghans and almost sold as a slave. He then served in the first Sikh War and progressed to civil administration in the Punjab, becoming one of the distinguished young men who served as political officers under the great Henry Lawrence. John served with his irregular troops alongside Sir Hugh Gough in the Second Sikh War, by which time his reputation among the native peoples for severe but fair administration won him deification. When the Indian Mutiny broke out in 1857 he took a leading part in suppressing the mutiny in the Punjab and then took command of his famous movable column which he led to the relief of Delhi.

In appearance he was like an Old Testament prophet, tall, massively built and with a huge black beard. His beliefs could be described as 'muscular Christianity' and his dislike of India and its people was so severe that his decision to spend his life in that country can only be understood by his determination to show them the benefits of Christianity. His personality was forceful and often humourless and he was a frightening companion, intolerant of weakness or failure. When asked by the Commissioner of the Punjab, Sir John Lawrence, to report on the punishments he was administering, he replied typically 'the punishment of mutiny is death.'

When the mutineers in Delhi heard from a spy that Nicholson's heavy siege guns were being brought down from the Punjab they sent an army of 6,000 men to capture them. But Nicholson also had his spies. On hearing that his guns were in danger, he set off in pursuit of the mutineers, defeating them utterly, killing 800 of the sepoys and capturing all their guns and baggage. After this the sepoys dared not leave their defences inside Delhi.

On 3 September Nicholson's heavy siege train reached Delhi and thereafter he could be seen day after day personally siting each gun on the ridge. Archdale Wilson resented the way that Nicholson was effectively usurping his command, disobeying orders and virtually bulldozing his way through all opposition, determined that nothing should interfere with the capture of the Moghul capital and the overthrow of the Mutiny. The problem was that Wilson insisted on playing a waiting game, while Nicholson preferred to storm the city without delay. As usual, Nicholson got his way. While his guns pounded Delhi's red stone walls until they crumbled, he organized the British troops into five columns, the first of which he would lead personally with the Gordon Highlanders and the best of his Punjab troops. Just 5,000 men were about to storm a city whose defences were still manned by well over 30,000 soldiers.

At dawn on 13 September, Nicholson led the first two columns, armed with scaling ladders, towards the breach that his guns had forced in the walls. In the early light of morning they faced a heartbreaking sight. During the night the mutineers had filled in the breach with sandbags and now the assault troops had to lie out in the open under the burning sun until the siege guns on the Ridge could reopen the breach. The sun was fully up by the time the breach was blown open again. At a signal from Nicholson the assault began once more. Soon hundreds of British and Sikh troops were tearing towards the red stone walls. However, they were in for a second shock. As they set up their ladders they found they were too short. Hundreds died as the mutineers poured a hail of bullets on them from the walls above. As the assault began to founder and his men fell back Nicholson stepped forward alone and began to tear the wall to pieces, stone by stone, ignoring the rocks that were thrown on him from above. Rejuvenated by this amazing sight, the assault troops returned to the walls and piled up rubbish and corpses on which to set the ladders. Nothing could stop them now. They swarmed up the ladders and were soon in possession of the walls.

While Nicholson was breaching the walls, the third column under Colonel Campbell were trying to force the Kashmir Gate. A 'forlorn hope' was sent forward to blow down the gate to allow the assault troops entry into the city. Showing unbelievable courage, for which they gained VCs, Lieutenants Home and Salkeld placed their explosive charges, packed them with sandbags and lit the fuses, all the while under a veritable rain of fire. A tremendous explosion wrecked the gate and to the sound of a trumpet the assault troops streamed through the smoke into the streets behind.

Once inside, the British troops found the fighting even harder. Every house held mutineers and every street had to be won step by step. John Nicholson was his usual impatient self. His forward troops began to drop back after suffering heavy casualties, but Nicholson believed himself invincible. He stepped out alone, just as he had under the walls of Delhi, and began to advance down one uncleared street until suddenly he spun round, shot in the right side by a sniper on the roof above. The wound was mortal but he did not want his men to see him fall. As in the case of the legendary El Cid, news of his wound was kept from the rank and file for fear that their morale would collapse.

So heavy were British casualties that General Archdale Wilson feared that he would lose his entire army in the streets and he contemplated withdrawal. But when the news reached the wounded Nicholson he tried to rise from his bed, threatening to shoot his commander. Eventually, Wilson realized that he was in too deep now to pull out. (Historically, British soldiers have a bad reputation when the subject of liquor is raised. At Badajoz in 1812 and at countless similar sieges in history drunken British soldiers, fighting like the Berserkers of old, have proved terrible foes to a stricken population. And in Delhi the British soldiers broke into the city wine merchants' premises and were soon forgetting the horrors of the fighting in a drunken stupor. For some 36 hours many of the British were incapacitated by drink but the mutineers took no advantage, most of them having made their escape from the city, which had become a death trap for them.)

Wilson now directed his attack on the Red Fort, in which some of the most determined sepoy militants were holding out. Lieutenant Home was again given the task of blowing the gates. Once again he was successful and the assault troops quickly despatched the garrison. With the fall of the Red Fort, Delhi was in

Burgoyne surrenders at Saratoga. His defeat was 'a thunderclap, which resounded round the world'.

The Battle of Albuera – the courage of the exceptional British troops, the 'Peninsula veterans', triumphed over the French despite the incompetence of their commander, Marshal Beresford.

Wellington – 'a master of defensive warfare' – is victorious over Marmont at the Battle of Salamanca.

The fighting at the Battle of Waterloo – Wellington triumphs over the Emperor Napoleon.

The charge of the guards at the Battle of Inkermann.

The Battle of Balaclava – the 'Charge of the Light Brigade'.

ABOVE: *The Siege of Delhi during the Indian Mutiny of 1857.*

BELOW: *The aftermath of Isandhlwana — the disastrous British defeat in the Zulu war*

ABOVE: *The Khalifa's standard is taken at Omdurman where Kitchener regained the Sudan and avenged the defeat of General Gordon.*

RIGHT: *The Battle of Spion Kop where inept generals squandered the lives of brave soldiers.*

ABOVE: *The Germans advance at Mons where British fire-power belied the Kaiser's description of Britain's 'contemptible little army'.*

RIGHT: *British troops going over the top on 1st July 1916 at the Battle of the Somme – 'the blackest day in the history of the British army'.*

ABOVE: *British stretcher-bearers carry a wounded soldier through the 'porridge of mud' of Passchendaele.*

Churchill commented 'Before Alamein we never had a victory. After Alamein we never had a defeat.'

British hands once again but at what cost. John Nicholson lived just long enough, like Wolfe at Quebec, to hear of victory. His statue that was built near the Kashmir Gate stood until India achieved independence in 1947. The Indian government then wanted to demolish it but – and this takes some believing – so fearsome had the man been in life that the superstitious Indians refused to dismantle it and instead shipped it to Ireland, where it stands today in his home town of Lisburn. Archdale Wilson, no hero but a dour commander who was essential to the success of the siege, was knighted and received a baronetcy along with a pension of £1,000 a year. Home, the explosives expert, was unfortunately killed just eleven days after the capture of the city. Of the British troops on the Ridge, known as the Delhi Field Force, 992 were killed and a further 2,795 were wounded. The number of mutineers who died in Delhi is impossible to compute. What is certain is that the British survivors so effectively pillaged the city that many returned to England as rich men.

24

The Battle of Isandhlwana
1879

The British never encountered the 'black Napoleon' himself, as Shaka, king of the Zulus, was described by early white settlers in Natal, South Africa; but in 1879 they faced the Frankenstein's monster that he had built – the Zulu army. Shaka it was who created the Zulu nation from a fairly insignificant Bantu tribe. By building a state based on a powerful army, he ensured that as British power spread throughout South Africa it would eventually have to reckon with the Zulu military system. The annexation of the Boer republic of Transvaal in 1877 was part of a British drive towards confederation in South Africa. But the peoples of the eastern territories of Natal and Transvaal could not rest while across the Tugela and Buffalo rivers a native despot of immense military potential ruled his kingdom according to his own whim and irrespective of British policy. In 1878 the British High Commissioner, Sir Bartle Frere, issued an ultimatum to the Zulu king, Cetshwayo, that he must disband his armies or face war with Britain. Cetshwayo was not eager for a war he knew he must lose, but to break up his armies was to give up his power as king, which he was unwilling to do. He refused the ultimatum and prepared to face the consequences.

The British commander in South Africa, Lord Chelmsford, invaded Zululand on 11 January 1879 with a mixed force of British and African troops sufficient, he believed, to win another one of the minor colonial wars at which the British were expert. He would have preferred more men but London had refused his request on the grounds of expense. Chelmsford, fresh from campaigning against the Gaikas, was unwittingly challenging one of the most efficient military systems ever developed outside Europe. The Zulus could raise as many as 60,000 warriors, who fought according to well-tried principles with weapons that made them more than equal to European troops in hand-to-hand combat. The endurance of Zulu warriors was legendary and over broken ground the British were to find to their cost that Zulus could outpace cavalry horses. In the aftermath of Isandhlwana many British survivors escaped the battlefield only to be hunted down before their horses could carry them to the Buffalo River crossing. The Zulus were not a military force to be underestimated, as the Boers tried to explain to the British regulars, but the latter had fought savages throughout the world and merely smiled knowingly.

Chelmsford began badly by dividing his command into three parts and entering Zululand with three separate columns, inviting the Zulus to destroy his army piecemeal. He commanded the central column himself, while his right column was under Colonel Pearson and his left under the very experienced Colonel Evelyn Wood. The idea was that the columns would unite at Cetshwayo's capital, Ulundi. Chelmsford crossed into Zululand at Rorke's Drift and camped near a hill called Isandhlwana. He had received every kind of warning from local Boers, who knew Zulu tactics and warned him of the speed with which a Zulu 'impi' could descend on him. However, Chelmsford was too professional a soldier to listen to civilian rumours. When his scouts reported that they had made contact with the enemy he further divided his forces by personally leading out half his central column to investigate, leaving the camp at Isandhlwana under the command of Lieutenant-Colonel Pulleine, with six companies of the 24th Regiment, South Wales Borderers and native troops from the Natal Native Contingent. Chelmsford was breaking just about every rule for fighting colonial wars, yet he could not envisage any danger and the arrogance of his officers reflected an unhealthy contempt for the enemy, usually a prelude to military disaster.

In their numerous wars against the Zulus the Boers had come to realize that only concentrated firepower, usually from behind laagered wagons, was enough to stop a Zulu charge. In close combat the Zulu was superior to his white opponent and therefore the most careful preparations should be made in Zulu country, to draw the wagons close together and supplement them with thorn bush. Chelmsford, in setting up camp, had not followed this wise policy and on the morning of 22 January, Pulleine faced an emergency with his troops distributed all over a hillside in small groups. It was an object lesson in how not to fight a 'Bush-war' against a savage opponent. While Chelmsford chased shadows with half his men, a large Zulu 'impi' of 20,000 warriors had given him the slip and closed in on the camp.

The battle that followed was surprisingly equal at first. The British regulars and their native allies had no chance, outnumbered as they were fifteen or twenty to one, yet at first the Zulus were toppled over in their hundreds by disciplined volleys. Charge after charge in various parts of the hillside was shattered by concentrated firepower. The courage of the Zulus was awesome, yet the desperation of the defenders gave them the edge at first. But it could not last long. The Zulus were breaking through in many places, getting round the back of the defenders and stabbing them with their assegais. And then occurred the curious incident that was to cost so many lives. As ammunition ran short men returned to the ammunition tents to collect enough for their sections. But none of the boxes had been opened ready for the engagement and their screws were rusty. Moreover, there were no screwdrivers available to open them. While men desperately held the stabbing Zulus at bay, urgent attempts were made in the tents to smash open the heavy boxes, with only partial success. Starved of ammunition, the British redcoats now saw their native allies break and run, allowing the Zulus to encircle them and move in for the kill. All order was lost and it was every man for himself.

The Zulus had been badly shaken by the combat so far. Never before had they faced such professional troops and such terrible firepower. Nevertheless, the day was theirs and they ruthlessly hunted down the few survivors. Meanwhile, a few miles away Chelmsford dismissed the sound of gunfire and the suggestion that his camp was under Zulu attack.

Isandhlwana was not a battle like the others described in this book. Inept leadership had given all the advantages to the Zulus and the men in the camp had been abandoned to a massacre. Yet the British soldier is often seen at his best in adversity and the flight to the Buffalo River contained great acts of heroism, for the Zulus were relentless pursuers. Lieutenants Melville and Coghill both were awarded posthumous Victoria Crosses for attempting to save the Queen's Colour as they crossed the Buffalo River. Altogether, 1,329 British and native troops died at Isandhlwana and probably at least 2,000 Zulus. It was the most crushing defeat a British army had suffered since the First Afghan War. Yet Cetshwayo did not glory in his victory. He knew that retribution would follow. And the Zulu losses at Isandhlwana and in the fighting at Rorke's Drift that followed the same day caused him agony. As he said, 'An assegai has been thrust into the belly of the nation. There are not enough tears to mourn the dead.' Zulu military power was finally broken by Chelmsford, ironically, at Ulundi in July 1879. But its swansong had been at Isandhlwana in January, greatest and last victory of the Zulu army built by Shaka in the early years of the century.

25

The Battle of Omdurman 1898

The death of General Gordon in Khartoum in 1885 was an enormous blow to national prestige and caused the fall of Gladstone's government in that year. *Punch* had referred to the British effort to save the general as 'Too little, too late,' and so for the next eleven years almost everyone in Britain waited to hear that the Sudan had been reconquered and Gordon avenged. Yet, when Britain eventually did decide to return to the Sudan, it had less to do with avenging Gordon than with preventing the French establishing themselves on the Upper Nile. It was Lord Salisbury's Conservative government of 1896 that decided to send an army down the Nile and the command of it was given to Herbert Kitchener, a man who had always admired Gordon. In fact it was a decision that was to make Kitchener's career, winning him a peerage and an international reputation.

It took the British thirty months to conquer the Sudan. It could have been done more quickly but Kitchener had no intention of going the same way as Gordon. He was an engineer trained at Woolwich, not a romantic like young Winston Churchill, who was to travel with the army. Kitchener's victory would be won before he even met the Dervish army and it would be a victory won by paddle steamers, locomotives and Maxim guns.

By September 1896 the Sirdar, an Egyptian title Kitchener carried as leader of an essentially Egyptian army, had laboriously cut his way through the desert to Dongola and here he spent twelve months before moving on to Berber, after building a new railway through the Nubian desert. But before Kitchener was prepared to make the final push to Khartoum he insisted that his army be reinforced by four further British battalions, a regiment of cavalry, all kinds of artillery, plus more engineers and an enlarged Army Medical Corps. He got everything he asked for, even including an infantry battalion from the Grenadier Guards. Kitchener intended to reconquer the Sudan in style. While the British troops played sports in the desert, notably fishing in the Nile while the officers went off on all manner of shooting expeditions, Kitchener brought his flotilla of gunboats up to strength. They were going to play a vital role in the campaign which, as Churchill called it, was essentially a river war.

At last, in March 1898, the Khalifa, who had succeeded to the temporal power of the Mahdi in the Sudan, decided to intervene. His son, Mahmud, was sent north with an army to Atbara, where he made it known that he intended to fight the British invaders. Mahmud built himself a strong position at Atbara, with trenches and a zariba (ring of thorn bushes) to protect the camp. But Kitchener took Mahmud's camp at the point of bayonet in just fifteen minutes. By August 1898 the extra troops from Britain had reached the Sudan and had been hastily transported by steamer to the vicinity of Omdurman. Kitchener now found himself in the comfortable position of having 25,000 men and 44 guns, as well as a flotilla of ten gunboats and five steamers for supplies and transport.

On reaching Omdurman, Kitchener allowed his gunners to fire on the Mahdi's tomb, which was covered by a great dome. A torrent of high explosive reduced the final resting place of Gordon's enemy to rubble. Kitchener was later to strew the bones of the holy man in the River Nile, keeping only the skull for an inkwell. Queen Victoria, on hearing of this desecration, hastily told him to put the skull back. The rest of the bones were not recovered. Yet Kitchener was more in touch with Victorian public opinion than the queen and it was a demonstration of his desire to avenge Gordon's death.

On 1 September the Dervish army moved out of Khartoum and drew up in battle array, part following the great black flag of the Khalifa and part following the banners of the Khalifa's son, Osman Sheik ed-Din. But apart from minor skirmishing there was no fighting that day. However, just after dawn the next day, 2 September, Kitchener's cavalry patrols reported that the Khalifa's army, amounting to perhaps 50,000 warriors, was on the move towards the British fortified camp, where Kitchener had drawn up his troops in a semi-circle, with each flank on the Nile. Behind the camp, and free to fire on the approaching horde from the river, were the gunboats. A war correspondent described the scene that followed: 'At first a few flags appeared over the crest, to be followed by solid masses of spearmen and riflemen, led by mounted Amirs. The muffled roar of a vast multitude reached the ears of the waiting Anglo-Egyptian Army as the Dervishes spread themselves in a gigantic semi-circle round the front and left of the position.'

At 6.50 a.m. the British field guns, supported by the massed artillery of the gunboats, opened fire on the dense ranks of the Dervish army, cutting huge swathes of dead and dying warriors but not slowing the advance. The Khalifa then ordered two divisions of about 14,000 men, led by Osman Digna and Osman Azrak, to charge straight at the British camp. When they were still over a mile away the British regulars opened fire with their modern rifles; at half a mile the British were joined by their Egyptian and Sudanese comrades with their older firearms. All the time the gunboats fired and the artillery tore gaps in the Dervish ranks. It was simply a massacre. Not a single Dervish reached within 500 yards of the British camp. Having slaughtered several thousand tribesmen in a few minutes, Kitchener's only comment was, 'What a dreadful waste of ammunition.'

After the defeat of the first Dervish attack, a second assault was made, aimed at the right flank of Kitchener's camp. Kitchener sent out his cavalry and the Egyptian Camel Corps but the latter proved unsuited to the rocky terrain. Fortunately for them, one of the gunboats on the river came to their aid, devastating the Dervishes as they closed in on them, killing more than 500 of them in a matter of seconds.

Kitchener now reached the mistaken conclusion that the battle was as good as over. Yet, unknown to him, the Khalifa had only so far used about a quarter of his force. The army of the Green Flag, some 20,000 strong, was somewhere to the north, while the Khalifa's own command, the army of the Black Flag, had also not come into action as yet. Convinced that he had won a complete victory, Kitchener ordered the 21st Lancers to pursue the beaten enemy. 'Annoy them as far as possible on their flank and head them off if possible from Omdurman,' ran the order to Colonel Martin, commander of the 21st. What happened next is as farcical as the Charge of the Light Brigade and almost as famous, thanks to the presence amongst the lancers of Winston Churchill.

Meanwhile, Kitchener decided to break camp, line up his brigades and march off towards Omdurman, exposing his flank to an enemy force of at least 40,000 men of whose exact whereabouts he was still completely ignorant. While Kitchener was tempting fate, Colonel Martin was looking for death or glory. The 21st had long suffered the scorn of the army as being the only regiment without any battle honours whatsoever and Martin was determined to change this at once. He was unlikely to win much fame for reconnoitring; nothing less than a full cavalry charge would do. Riding to the front and issuing the order to charge, Martin led his 400 officers and troopers in a mad, wonderful, charge across the desert sands towards a thin line of Dervishes. But as he breasted a rise he suddenly found to his horror that he had ridden into a force of 2,000 Dervish warriors commanded by Osman Digna and concealed in a dry watercourse. In the next two minutes of hacking and slashing that followed five officers, 65 men and 119 horses were killed or wounded. Martin rode back to report to Kitchener that he had carved himself a tiny niche in military history, as leading the last cavalry charge by the British army. For his failure to follow orders Martin was made a Companion of the Bath and three of his men got VCs.

Meanwhile, the two foremost British infantry brigades had formed up and marched out of the camp towards Omdurman. There was almost a holiday spirit now that the battle was over and the brigades vied with each other to be first to reach the enemy capital. Unfortunately, as the other brigades followed in line no one gave much thought to the rearmost brigade, an Egyptian one, commanded by Brigadier-General Hector MacDonald, a tough, God-fearing Highland officer, who was said to have knocked out a Boer at the battle of Majuba Hill with a straight right punch. Unknown to Kitchener, MacDonald was about to be attacked by fully 40,000 Dervishes, from the armies of the Green and the Black Flags. Attacked from both sides, MacDonald sent Lieutenant Pritchard to tell Kitchener of his parlous position and two brigades were immediately sent to MacDonald's aid. But for a while all that stood between Kitchener and a total disaster was MacDonald's brigade of Egyptian troops. As the Dervishes made attack after attack on MacDonald's men, the Scot held them together with an astonishing display of leadership, riding out in front of them and coolly controlling their fire until he had broken the final Dervisher assault. If there was a hero at Omdurmann it was Hector MacDonald.

At 11.30 a.m. Kitchener closed his glasses and announced that the enemy had been given 'a good dusting'. This was an understatement. Nearly 11,000 Dervish bodies were counted on the battlefield, and as many as 16,000 others were wounded, some of whom died later of gangrene, for the British were using dum-dum bullets, which inflicted terrible exit wounds. It had been one of the great killings in African history and orders had been given to shoot any wounded tribesmen who looked dangerous. After the battle the Khalifa's black banner was brought to Kitchener by Captain Henry Rawlinson (later to command the 4th Army in the battle of the Somme in 1916). The Khalifa himself escaped from Omdurman and was not located until 24 November 1899, when he was killed by Sir Reginald Wingate's pursuing forces.

Two days after the battle, representatives of every regiment in the battle paraded in front of Gordon's ruined palace at Khartoum. The national anthems of Britain and Egypt were played, a 21-gun salute was fired and the hymn 'Abide with me' (Gordon's favourite) was sung. Gordon was avenged in a way that warmed the hearts of Victorian Britain. Sudan was British once again.

26

The Battle of Spion Kop 1900

Just as the Crimean War has become infamous in British history for the appalling conditions in which the British army was forced to fight, so the Second Boer War has become associated with the very poor standard of British generalship. In the early weeks of the war in South Africa Britain lost battle after battle to the Boers who out-shot, outrode and outfought their professional opponents. The battle of Spion Kop is just one example of how inept generals can squander the lives of brave soldiers. Ironically, just as in 1898 Winston Churchill took part in the battle of Omdurman in the Sudan, he was also present at Spion Kop in South Africa two years later as a war correspondent, and witnessed British failure at first hand.

In the early months of the Boer War the British commander, Sir Redvers Buller, made strenuous attempts to relieve the Boer siege of Ladysmith. But his progress towards the town was held up by fierce Boer resistance, which inflicted on Buller a full-scale defeat at Colenso. Three weeks later, reinforced by a new division under Sir Charles Warren – curiously, the police commissioner who had failed to trap Jack the Ripper was now a 59-year-old general, who had been on the retired list for a year – Buller was ready to try again, this time with Warren's 5th Division, which brought British strength up to 30,000 regulars. It sounded an impressive force but how was Buller to employ so many men against so mobile an opponent? The problem was Warren himself, whom Buller referred to as 'the dug-out ex-policeman'. In February 1900, while the fight-ing raged around Hussar Hill, Warren took a bath in public to entertain his troops. Buller was appalled to find his colleague demeaning himself and the reputation of the British army in this way and was constantly worried by Warren's 'fads and fancies'. There are grounds for doubting Warren's sanity, yet Buller, for all that he thought Warren mad, gave him command of the assault on Spion Kop, the key to the the Boer positions guarding the route to Ladysmith. Why Buller preferred instead to look on and to act as 'an umpire at manoeuvres' is difficult to understand. In the event neither Buller nor Warren ordered a proper reconnaissance of the area, and simply ordered troops to occupy the hill known as Spion Kop. What they were to do after that they were never told. To head the assault of the hill, which was a strenuous climb of nearly 1,500 feet, Warren selected General Talbot-Coke, who was suffering from a recently broken leg. Buller did question this and Warren replaced Talbot-Coke with the 55-year-old General Woodgate.

In planning the assault it did not occur to Warren to send up machine guns to increase the British firepower, or a field telegraph unit to keep him in touch with the men on the hill. As a result, once on the hill, the troops would be completely out of contact with him and unable to react to his orders. Sandbags had been prepared to fortify the top but they were left behind, and just 20 picks and shovels were taken to entrench 2,000 men. Moreover, while this small force engaged the entire Boer strength, more than 20,000 troops encamped at the base of the hill doing precisely nothing.

In thick fog the assault troops, mainly from the Lancashire Brigade, set off up the rocky slopes of the hill, led by Colonel Thorneycroft, while the rest of the army simply stood and watched. As the younger and fitter men pulled ahead, Woodgate fell further behind until he was being almost carried. His men, told to empty their rifles and use the bayonet alone reached what they took to be the summit and began to try to dig themselves in, only to find their spades striking solid rock. As visibility began to improve they received a shock; they were not at the top at all but on a sort of plateau some way from the actual peak. Higher up there were three better positions which the British troops could have occupied, but the Boers got there first and opened fire on Woodgate's men from three sides. Trapped on a plateau no more than a quarter of a mile square and without proper cover, the British troops were helpless in the face of a heavy and accurate fire from Boer sharpshooters. As at Majuba Hill in 1881, and against the same opponents, some of the British troops fought with great heroism while others simply surrendered.

The Battle of Spion Kop 1900

When Winston Churchill, in his capacity as a war correspondent, tried to persuade General Warren that his men were trapped on Spion Kop, the general flew into a rage and ordered his arrest. On Spion Kop itself General Woodgate had been mortally wounded and Colonel Thorneycroft had taken over command. But for nine hours Thorneycroft got no instructions from Warren, and eventually he ordered a withdrawal from the hill. Ironically, Warren had at last decided to occupy the hill in force. As Thorneycroft's survivors clambered down the slopes they met fresh troops climbing up to meet them. But it was too late. The Boers were still masters of Spion Kop and Warren was forced to call off the entire operation. Ironically, the Boers had suffered losses themselves in the heavy exchange of fire and had also decided to abandon the hill. Thus as the British retreated down one side of Spion Kop, the Boers were climbing down the other, leaving the hill unoccupied except for the dead. The British had lost heavily, leaving behind 300 dead and suffering 1,200 casualties in total. British officers on the hill had suffered 62 per cent casualties. Although the Boers' casualties had been just a quarter of the British, they could afford them less. Nevertheless, when the Boer commander Louis Botha realized that Spion Kop was unoccupied he reacted faster than the British commanders and rushed new troops to the top. As day dawned the Boers were back where they had been the previous day and the British had suffered another humiliating defeat.

The battle of Spion Kop deserves a place in any book of military incompetence. Few of the British commanders emerged with any credit; one was perhaps Thorneycroft who had fought heroically all day, but Warren was simply out of his depth. A foolish belief in the bayonet as a weapon meant that the British assault troops did not take with them the necessary artillery, machine guns, entrenching tools, food or water to enable them to hold the hill for any length of time. In the aftermath, Buller did not have to look far for a scapegoat. As he wrote to his wife, 'We were fighting all last week but old Warren is a duffer and lost me a good chance.' Yet it was Buller who was really to blame for giving Warren charge of the battle when he was obviously incompetent. From now on even Buller's most faithful supporters began to call him 'Sir Reverse Buller'.

27

The Battle of Mons 1914

German contempt for the British army was well established in the fifty years prior to the First World War. On being asked what he would do if the British army landed on the Baltic coast Prince Bismarck remarked that he would send the local police to arrest it. Certainly what the German military observers saw of the Tommies in the Boer Wars in South Africa only confirmed what they thought, which was that the soldiers were courageous amateurs led by ridiculous fun-loving aristocrats who thought more of sport than of war. As usual with such observations there was more than a grain of truth in it. Yet, if the Germans had seen the concentration on speed and accuracy of rifle fire that was a vital part of the training of British soldiers immediately before 1914, the smile would have died on their lips. There may have been just 100,000 in the British Expeditionary Force sent to France, compared to the millions of conscript soldiers who made up the German, French, Russian and Austrian armies, but the Tommies were by far the best troops in the world in August 1914. The Germans were going to have to learn this the hard way in the Belgian industrial town of Mons.

In 1914 the Germans had placed all their hopes for a quick victory on the famous Schlieffen Plan, a massive 'hook' by five German armies which were to pass through Belgium, Artois, Picardy and then to the west of Paris before crushing the French against the remaining German armies in Lorraine. However, by violating Belgian neutrality the Germans unexpectedly brought Britain into the war alongside France, and by an irony of fate it was to be the tiny British army that was to administer the *coup de grâce* to German hopes on the Marne in September 1914.

The Schlieffen Plan was a brilliant but flawed concept, aimed at avoiding the old Prussian strategic nightmare – a war on two fronts. The German High Command expected to win the war in the west in six weeks, before moving German forces east to deal with the Russians, who, it was thought, would be slow to mobilize. But the plan was built around a fatal error. Simple mathematics should have shown the German planners that General Alexander von Kluck's 1st Army, on the extreme right of the German 'hook', would have to travel much further – and much faster – than the Crown Prince's 5th Army on the inside of the wheel. Any delays encountered by von Kluck from unexpected Belgian – or British – resistance could be disastrous. In the event, it was resistance by the British Expeditionary Force (BEF) at Mons and Le Câteau that disrupted the German timetable and cost the Germans the swift victory around which they had built all their planning.

The BEF crossed the Channel during 11–18 August 1914 without losing a single man. They came by night for fear of U-boats, landing at Boulogne, Rouen and Le Havre, and moving forward to their assembly point at Maubeuge, not far from the Belgian border. The first four divisions to arrive were more a token of support for the great French army and did not expect to be plunged straight into action. As a flank guard to the French they expected to be on the extreme left of the front, virtually brushing the seashore with their left sleeves. Unfortunately, of course, they were in just the place that von Schlieffen had planned that the German soldier on the extreme right of their wheel would brush the Channel with his right sleeve. At first the French simply refused to believe that the Germans were seriously intending to come through Belgium; they still expected the main battle to be in Lorraine. As a result, the British found themselves occupying an area of supreme importance to the survival of France. If they cracked, Paris would fall and with it probably France as well.

The summer weather was splendid as the British troops marched northwards across the Belgian border. They were to take up positions on the left flank of General Lanrezac's 5th Army. At this stage the war still had an unreal quality yet not far ahead, on 20 August, the Belgian army had been defeated and the Germans had occupied Brussels. That same day a Royal Flying Corps reconaissance plane reported that it had sighted masses of German troops marching through Louvain. Marshal Joffre, the French commander-in-chief, ordered Lanrezac to advance and stem the German tide and where he went the BEF was obliged to go.

The British troops moved up to the Belgian industrial town of Mons, just as their ancestors had done under the command of Marlborough and Wellington. Their surroundings were strange, to say the least. The British had never before fought in the middle of a town, with the local population going about its normal daily existence. Tommies found themselves in back gardens with washing hanging from lines and flapping around them in the breeze. All around them were factories, slag-heaps, mines and pitheads. It was known as Belgium's 'Black country' and war there would contradict every military textbook ever written. Still, British officers reasoned, once the French had got the Germans on the run, the whole Allied line would be able to advance and leave these black-faced Belgian miners to their own devices. But the French under Lanrezac were already in action against von Kluck's 1st Army and they were being driven back. Meanwhile, the first two British casualties of the war had occurred, two men killed by mistake by British pickets. It was a bad start.

The British commander-in-chief, Sir John French, had moved his headquarters up to Le Câteau. He was still at ease with the world, supremely confident in the strength and traditions of the French army. Later that day his mood was bleaker when the British liaison officer with Lanrezac, Lieutenant Spears, brought news that the French were beaten and in full retreat. Only the BEF stood between the German 1st Army and a complete breakthrough. Lanrezac was relying on the British now to cover his retreat. Yet how could the four divisions of British troops hold back the 320,000 Germans when a whole French army had failed? Fortunately for Lanrezac and indeed for the whole Entente, the British, outnumbered more than three to one, were displaying their usual 'sublime stupidity'. General French assured Lanrezac that the BEF would stop the Germans at Mons and would guarantee to hold them back for 24 hours, which would allow him to make his escape.

The British were still amateurs at war, as the Germans claimed. One young officer failed to set up an outpost at Mons to cover the German advance on the grounds that the enemy would not come from a certain direction as it was private property. The Germans, who had just torched the great medieval city of Louvain, destroying its world-famous library in the process, would scarcely have credited such naivety. They were under direct orders from Kaiser Wilhelm II 'to exterminate the treacherous English and walk over General French's contemptible little army'.

The leading British troops were digging in along the Mons-Condé Canal and as the sun rose on 23 August it was these men who first encountered the Germans. Both sides were in for a shock. The Germans had assumed that the British were in retreat with the French and were astonished to find themselves facing determined opposition. Nevertheless, they advanced towards the British lines with undiminished confidence. And then the British opened fire and it was like the arrow storm at Crécy all over again. As one British soldier described: 'The Germans were in solid square blocks, standing out sharply against the skyline, and you couldn't help hitting them.' The speed and accuracy of the British firing – 15 aimed shots a minute – shattered the German advance, killing hundreds of men in a matter of seconds. So shocked were the German officers that they assumed that the British were firing massed machine guns at them. In fact, the British fired hardly any machine-guns for the simple reason that they had virtually none with them. So effective was the British rifle fire that the Germans were now forced to bring up artillery to support their infantry. And now the tables began to turn. The Tommies were inundated with heavy shells and, gallingly, there were no British guns to return fire. As soon as they thought the British had got their heads down the German infantry came pouring forward again, only to be met by the same invincible rifle fire. Corporal Holbrook of the Royal Fusiliers described what it was like: 'You couldn't see the earth for them there were that many. Time after time they gave the order 'Rapid Fire'. Well, you didn't wait for the order, really! You'd see a lot of them coming in a mass on the other side of the canal and you just let them have it . . . They didn't get anywhere near us with this rapid fire.' The impact of British firepower on the German infantry was devastating. Probably never again in the entire war were German lives thrown away so cheaply and the superiority of the British soldier so clearly illustrated.

Even at this early stage in the war, the Germans were hammering home that this was to be an artillery war, and soon the forward British positions were simply wiped out. Quick to exploit their artillery's success, the German infantry had crossed the canal and was driving the British through Mons. And yet the slaughter of the German infantry went on all the time. Facing the Royal West Kents at St Ghislain were the Brandenburg Grenadiers, who marched forward in a tight unit singing *Deutschland über Alles*, and all the time the Kents kept firing and slaughtering more and more of them. It was less like a battle than target-shooting at Bisley.

The BEF eventually withdrew from Mons, having suffered 1,600 casualties from the 12 battalions engaged. The German casualties were enormous, yet were readily accepted by their officers in what they assumed was a war-winning advance. Nevertheless, the British had fought the Germans to a standstill and both sides needed to rest and recuperate. But while the Germans buried their dead, there was no rest for the Tommies. The BEF began its long retreat from Mons. The Tommies had only been in France for ten days at the most and in that time they had felt the full gamut of emotions, from elation to depression. Having slaughtered the Germans by the thousand, they now found themselves running away. As they marched through one French town they found themselves, ironically, trampling on a banner that had hung across the street on their arrival. It read, 'Welcome to the Tommies'. It was not until 2 September that the British troops reached safety behind the River Marne.

28

The Battle of the Somme 1916

The flood of volunteers to fight for 'King and Country' in response to Field Marshal Kitchener's appeal in 1914 was both spontaneous and genuinely patriotic. The British people, along with Kitchener alone of all politicians and generals, seemed to realize the immense struggle that was about to ensue. A modern war between industrial nations would not end quickly. Upper-class Britons might be joining up so as not to 'miss the fun' and be promising their loved ones that 'it'll all be over by Christmas', but Kitchener was preparing for a long, attritional war, in which the masses would provide the nation's military sinew rather than a few Guardsmen with lances, fresh from chasing foxes or seeking to act out their dreams of glory. It was from the industrial cities of Northern Britain that the nation's lifeblood came and Kitchener responded to the enthusiasm of Northern working men by allowing volunteers to choose their own titles for their units, join up with their friends and colleagues, and serve together in the same battalion. This was the beginning of the 'Pals battalions'.

The idea that had originated in the North of England caught on elsewhere. Soon 'Pals' units were blossoming throughout the country. From Welsh holiday resorts to London slum boroughs, men poured forth in their battalions with the unlikely names of the First Public Works Battalion, the Forest of Dean Pioneers, the Civil Service Battalion, the Grimsby Chums, the North-East Railway Battalion, the Artists and Writers' Battalion. Even 'Bantam' units were set up for the miners, many of whom, though tough as nails, were very short and much below the minimum height allowed for normal regiments. One of the most tragic methods of selecting new officers was that of preparing a list of 2,000 'young gentlemen' who had just left the best of England's schools or universities. These young men were immediately offered a commission simply on the assumption that men from their background – educationally, socially and financially – would inevitably be 'officer material'. Courage these youngsters had in buckets but of common sense or even natural caution they had little. The great schools of England – Eton, Winchester, Harrow, Westminster, Rugby, Charterhouse, Marlborough, Wellington and their like – all contributed their sixth-form leavers willingly. And each of these schools and hundreds like them today boasts its well-oiled plaques recording those who died in the Great War 'For King and Country'.

To the recruits, with their dummy rifles and blue serge uniforms, it all seemed like a great adventure. Without accommodation in barracks, many of the 'Pals' had to live at home. Each day they would assemble in a field or on a hillside and train to be soldiers, dressed in their civilian clothes and carrying broomsticks for guns. They were 'Kitchener's Army' and they were intensely proud. But in a sense the happiness was borne of ignorance.

None of these volunteers saw action until 1 July 1916 and after that day nothing could ever be the same again: it was the blackest day in the history of the British army. It was a day that ended forever the idea that British infantry possessed the moral advantage over their enemies that they believed had been theirs by right since the days of Minden in the eighteenth century. The Boer War had severely dented this belief but after the BEF's heroic displays at Mons and First Ypres, there were those who believed that the sight of British troops in line abreast marching towards them was still enough to put any enemy to flight. The Germans were never subscribers to this whimsical British conviction. They were the professionals, the British clearly the 'amateurs'. And among the 60,000 casualties the British incurred on 1 July, many who fell were from the 'Pals' battalions, enthusiastic but half-trained civilians, fighting and dying with their friends for company.

The architects of 1 July – for there were two – were Sir Douglas Haig, the British commander-in-chief and Sir Henry Rawlinson, commander of the British 4th Army. On 1 July 1916, Rawlinson, in fact, was commanding probably the biggest army –

the 4th Army had over 500,000 men – that any British general had ever commanded. The great responsibility, unfortunately, seemed to reveal cracks in his own moral courage. He had been given a priceless gift by his country – a huge army of British volunteers – with which to launch what was hoped would be the war-winning offensive against the Germans. But was Rawlinson – or indeed Haig – man enough to use it?

The strategic situation in 1916 required a 'grand gesture' by Britain, if only to demonstrate to her allies that she was prepared to bear her share of the common burden. By the end of 1915 it had become apparent to the British Government that there was no prospect of the war against the Central Powers being won without Britain assuming a much greater share of the fighting. French losses in their spring and autumn offensives of 1915 had stretched their manpower to its limits. It was obvious that the vast numbers of Britons who had responded to Lord Kitchener's appeal for volunteers in 1914 would now need to be used in France. Thus, when the Allies met at Chantilly to coordinate their strategy for 1916, Britain was obliged to commit herself to a summer offensive in France, in conjunction with a major French offensive there.

On 7 April 1916 the British Government authorized their new commander-in-chief, Sir Douglas Haig, to concert an offensive with the French. The battlefield was to be the Somme region, a poor choice. The German front lines there enjoyed the advantage of the high ground, so that the lines of British soldiers advancing would face a climb towards the strategically vital Pozières ridge. In addition, the chalky subsoil had allowed the Germans, who had held the area since October 1914, to construct intricate and effective underground defences, resistant to artillery barrage. The Somme was the choice of French commander Marshal Joseph Joffre, and Haig felt obliged to comply. At first, Joffre had planned an operation in which equal numbers of French and British troops would be involved, but after the Germans began their massive assault on Verdun the French commitment to the Somme diminished. Joffre was only able to offer 13 divisions to support the 20 or so British divisions earmarked for the assault.

Previous British offensives at Loos and Neuve Chapelle in 1915 had demonstrated that unsupported infantry and cavalry had no chance in the contested zone while enemy firepower remained unsuppressed. On the Somme, therefore, it would be necessary to overwhelm the German defences with an artillery bombardment of unprecedented weight and ferocity. Once the artillery had succeeded in demolishing the enemy, it would be a relatively simple task for the infantry to occupy the ground won.

With the French on its right, Rawlinson's 4th Army was to attack along an 18-mile front between Gommecourt in the north and Montauban in the south. Half a million men under his command would prepare the most prodigious military operation ever undertaken by a British army. In some ways Rawlinson – an efficient administrator and an effective infantry general – was a good choice, yet in one vital element he did not see eye-to-eye with Haig about the forthcoming battle.

Haig and Rawlinson were at odds with each other as to what exactly was the aim of the offensive. Haig was still thinking in terms of a 'decisive battle' which would break the German lines and enable him to use his massed cavalry corps to burst through into open ground. Thus Haig hoped to punch a hole and pour through it in a grand Napoleonic sweep. Unfortunately for him, and perhaps for his men, Rawlinson did not agree with him. He had lost hope of a breakthrough and preferred to think in terms of a 'bite and hold' operation. He rejected Haig's belief in 'going for the big thing' and, instead, aimed to deliver against limited targets sharp blows intended to exhaust the German reserves as they tried to repair holes at various points in their line.

A staggering amount of preparation was needed behind the British lines in the weeks before the operation was to take place. Hundreds of thousands of horses and transport vehicles passed endlessly up the newly constructed roads and railways, and field guns, howitzers and mortars in unprecedented quantities were moved into position and hidden from prying German eyes. But secrecy was impossible and the Germans were quite prepared for the British attack when it came.

As a professional soldier, Rawlinson seemed to have little faith in the men who would compose the assault force on 1 July. Sixty per cent of them would be men from Kitchener's 'New Army', who in his eyes could not be trusted to do anything properly. As a result, whereas the French infantry on the British right advanced across no man's land in small, tight groups, rushing from one piece of dead ground to another, covered all the time by other groups behind them, the British soldiers, each weighed down by 70 pounds of equipment, were ordered to advance upright, a yard or two apart from their neighbours and at a walking pace, to prevent them panicking and diving for cover. A training memorandum issued just three weeks before the attack by Haig's Chief of Staff, Sir Lancelot Kiggell, ordered the attacking infantry to advance in four rows. The German defenders were later to write in astonishment about the slow, steady march of the British who, had they come at a rush, would certainly have succeeded in capturing many more trenches.

Rawlinson's tactics were a formula for disaster and one might, at this stage, be wondering how such absurd instructions were ever given to soldiers marching in some places as far as a thousand yards into barbed wire, all the time under raking fire from machine guns. In his own defence, Rawlinson would have insisted that this scenario was wrong for the simple reason that there would not be any machine guns, or barbed wire, or even live Germans. The British infantry was advancing to occupy ground won for it by the devastating weight of the British bombardment. And in this assumption lay the core of the disaster that was to strike the 4th Army on 1 July 1916.

Rawlinson's confidence in the power and effectiveness of his artillery was absolute. As he told his officers, 'Nothing could exist at the conclusion of the bombardment in the area covered by it.' He was using 1,437 guns on a fifteen-mile front and his guns would suppress German artillery fire when the assault began, destroy the German barbed wire, even though some of it was so thick that light could scarcely pass through its close-meshed coils; and his guns would kill all the German soldiers in their trenches, dug-outs and bunkers. So there would be no one left alive to scythe down the walking waves of 4th Army. But just how effective would the British bombardment be? Previous barrages had only ever succeeded where the Germans were taken by surprise or had poor bunkers in unsuitable terrain. But the Germans had been in their Somme positions for two years and had used the time to build the best and deepest defensive positions on the whole of the Western Front. In places the British would meet four separate trench systems and might have to cross twelve trenches before reaching open country. Concrete dug-outs thirty feet deep kept the soldiers in safety during the barrage, and barbed wire entanglements of awesome efficiency lined the forward trenches.

Rawlinson's confidence in the guns was quite misplaced. Of the 1,437 artillery pieces available, only 467 were heavy guns and of those just 34 were of 9.2 inch calibre or more. In the event, just 30 tons of explosive were to fall on each mile of the German front, hardly impressive when the distinguished military historian John Keegan has suggested that such powerful defences would today warrant several small nuclear warheads. Even worse was the nature of the shells that would be fired. Nearly two-thirds would be shrapnel, deadly to men in the open, but harmless to those in deep dugouts. Of the 12,000 tons of explosive fired by British guns in the last week of June, 1916, just 900 tons were of high explosive capable of destroying the deepest German defences.

The failure of the artillery bombardment presented Haig and Rawlinson with a fundamental choice: cancel the operation or go ahead in the knowledge that they were sending their men to certain death. Unfortunately, both generals lacked the moral courage necessary to take the first option. In spite of intelligence reports that spoke of unbroken barbed wire facing three of the five corps due to attack on 1 July, and of German prisoners taken who had clearly suffered little from the intensive barrage, they decided to go on with the operation. Haig even remarked fatuously, 'The barbed wire has never been so well cut, nor the artillery preparations so thorough.' Rawlinson agonized: 'I am not quite satisfied that all the wire has been thoroughly well cut and in places the front trench is not knocked about as I should like to see in the photos. The bit in front of the 34th Division has been rather let off.' In fact, it was the 34th Division that was to be massacred on 1 July. With the evidence to hand, Rawlinson could have prevented this, but he did not, ordering the attack to proceed as if the barrage had been totally successful.

The men were told deliberate lies to maintain morale. The Sherwood Foresters were assured: 'You will meet nothing but dead and wounded Germans. You will advance on Mouquet Farm and be there by 11 A.M. The field kitchens will follow you and give you a good meal.' The King's Own Yorkshire Light Infantry (who were to suffer 76 per cent casualties) were told: 'When you go over the top, you can slope arms, light up your pipes and cigarettes, and march all the way to Pozières before meeting any live Germans.'

At 7.30 a.m. on 1 July the first waves of 60,000 men went over the top and marched slowly towards the German lines. Some were led by officers who kicked footballs, others by men with walking sticks or umbrellas. It was a jaunt, they had been told. Captain W.P. Nevill of the 8th East Surreys had purchased four footballs while home on leave and provided one to each of his platoons. He offered a prize to the first of his platoons that managed to kick their ball into the German trenches. One of his young lieutenants even inscribed his ball with the message:

> The Great European Cup
> The Final
> East Surreys v. Bavarians
> Kick Off at Zero

At zero hour Nevill's men punted their footballs into no man's land and hurtled after them. (One of these footballs is preserved in the National Army Museum.) Nevill was never able to present his prize to the winners: he was killed, shortly after kicking off for one of his platoons.

Within 30 minutes of zero hour half of the British assault troops had become casualties. Of the 120,000 from 143 battalions who attacked that day nearly 60,000 casualties were suffered, including some 20,000 dead. It was the greatest loss ever suffered by the British army and the heaviest by any army in a single day of the entire war. In fact, British battle casualties that day exceeded those from the entire Crimean War, Boer War and Korean War put together. The German soldiers had survived the barrage in their deep concrete bunkers and, warned by the cessation of the bombardment ten minutes before zero hour they emerged to the sound of bugles from below ground and reached their machine guns before the slowly advancing British troops were even halfway across no man's land. In those areas where the British did succeed in taking German positions, they found them intact and even with the electric lights still working.

The British troops were met by not just rifle- and machine-gun fire, they also marched into the face of a counter-barrage from the German artillery, which had similarly survived Rawlinson's bombardment. Even where the wire had been broken the passages created served as death-traps, for the Germans had concentrated their firepower on these openings. Elsewhere, the wire trapped thousands of men, equipped only with pitiful hand-cutters, who could find no way through and milled about like flocks of sheep until the machine guns scythed them down. One battalion of the Newfoundland Regiment suffered 91 per cent casualties on the wire.

The regiments which suffered worst contained the 'Pals' battalions. As wounded men began to stream back, anxious battalion commanders in the second wave telephoned for new orders but the answer was always, 'You must stick to your plan. You must carry out orders.' On the left of the advance, around Gommecourt and Beaumont Hamel, the British made no progress at all and suffered dreadful casualties. In the centre, behind which Gough's Reserve Army of three cavalry and two infantry divisions was massed, some progress was made but successes were isolated. Even where German trenches were taken the forward troops could not communicate with the British lines to tell them of their success as runners were shot down in hundreds and telephone wires cut by artillery fire. Only on the right, where better French tactics prevailed, was real progress made. The Germans were taken by surprise here, for they had not expected the French to be able to launch an attack in view of their recent martyrdom in the great struggle around Verdun.

By the end of the day the British held a three-mile-wide portion of the German position, to a depth of one mile, and just three of the thirteen target villages. At no point had they reached the second line of German defences. Rawlinson had more reason to be pleased than Haig; his men were at least 'holding' a small sector, but it had been achieved at the cost of nearly eight casualties for every one German. Haig blithely commented that the casualties could not be considered severe in view of the numbers engaged.

No previous army commander with such casualties had ever expressed himself satisfied. Haig's complete ignorance of events was clearly demonstrated by his attribution of cowardice to Hunter-Weston's 8th Corps. In Haig's words, 'few of the VIII Corps even left their trenches'. In fact, 8th Corps suffered over 13,000 casualties, the highest of any corps involved. And what was awaiting the casualties who were lucky enough to be brought back from the front? Between Albert and Amiens a casualty clearing station had been set up to expect 1,000 casualties. Within a few hours of the start of the battle they were overwhelmed by 10,000 wounded men. A surgeon there wrote of 'streams of ambulances a mile long' waiting to be unloaded.

The five months of fighting on the Somme saw the most bitter attritional battle not just of the First World War but in all history. The British and the Germans fired over thirty million shells at each other and suffered in return over a million casualties in an area little more than seven square miles in extent. The drama of 1 July was to remain unmatched by later events, yet the battle went on. Tanks were used by the British on 15 September for the first time in the history of warfare but they were too few to prove decisive. In the grim weather of November the battle was finally brought to a close. Haig was able to claim a victory of sorts, but at what cost. Yet – in Haig's defence – the Germans with hindsight believe that it was in the Somme fighting that the old German army died.

29

The Battle of Passchendaele 1917

The third battle of Ypres, more commonly known as Passchendaele, holds a special place in the memories of most First World War soldiers. It is generally regarded as the most dreadful as well as the most pointless exercise in the futility of war. Fought in the worst conditions for a target that was hardly worth the bones of a Coldstream Guardsman, it is well summed up by the reaction of a staff officer who visited the front after four months of fighting. As his car approached the battle area he became increasingly uneasy at the swamplike conditions. 'Good God, did we really send men to fight in that?' he asked the driver, bursting into tears. 'That's nothing,' the driver replied, 'It's far worse further up.'

The British had known for some time that the German defences at Passchendaele were very strong. Intelligence reports since autumn 1916 had reported unusual German activity in the area and half a million aerial photographs of the area showed every possible detail of the German defences. But this posed a serious problem for the British High Command. To break down the German defences there would need to be a heavy preliminary bombardment, even greater than that used on the Somme. As the area was close to sea level it would flood very easily. Once the big guns had churned up the ground the area would be impassable for tanks, leaving the infantry to slog through the slime on their own. Yet Haig was dangerously optimistic. If the weather stayed dry, he reasoned, it just might be done. But if it rained, the whole front would soon become impossible. He therefore had the weather charts for the region checked and rechecked. Over the previous thirty years July and August had been unpredictable months with occasional heavy thunderstorms. But September was usually good, so if you were lucky and had a fine July and August you might have a stretch of twelve dry weeks. But that was as much as you could expect, for October was the wettest month of the year. Any campaign that began in July must not go on beyond September. Once started, the battle must be concluded quickly; there could be no long drawn-out attrition as on the Somme in 1916. Appreciating the need for quick action, Haig chose the 'dashing' Hubert Gough to spearhead the assault rather than the more reliable but ponderous Plumer, victor at Messines.

The British bombardment opened on 22 July and lasted for ten days. On the last day of July, in heavy rain, twelve infantry divisions attacked along an eleven-mile front. Progress was slow. Two weeks later a replica of the first attack was made but again progress was almost imperceptible and conditions were becoming so bad that operations had to be halted. British infantry operations were more amphibious than terrestrial. As they sank into the swamp the Tommies provided easy targets for the German machine-guns, firing from their massive concrete bunkers. Haig was beginning to doubt the wisdom of going on. His only chance had been a quick breakthrough. If only he could have accepted that he was wrong and called off the operation before too much damage was done. All that he was left with was the chance of a 'slogging-match' like the Somme, but worse. Were the British in condition to fight an attritional battle so soon after the Somme? The answer should have been a resounding 'no'. Why did Haig lack the courage to admit it?

First there was the problem of numbers. By the end of 1917 – with the expected defeat of Russia – Germany could expect to transfer as many as twenty new divisions to the Western front. Intelligence reports also indicated that the Germans had a million men in training depots and a further two million available should they require them. All this had to be set against a British shortfall of 60,000 men in France and Lord Derby's startling revelation that British manpower was already 'at bedrock'. Derby made it absolutely clear to Haig that manpower must be conserved at all costs. This was hardly the support that Haig needed if he was planning another attritional battle. Even British divisions in the line in the summer of 1917 were often up to 4,000 men below strength. Haig was already falsifying the statistics by clearing V.D. hospitals and ordering lightly wounded men back to the front. In London ministers were becoming very suspicious of Haig's low casualty returns.

Yet if the manpower situation was so serious why did Haig persevere with the Passchendaele offensive after it had demonstrably failed to achieve a quick breakthrough? Clearly, he did not have the human resources for a long drawn-out battle and so why did Lloyd George not stop him – even sack him? The truth lies in the realm of grand strategy. Britain was aware that Germany had made peace offers to France, but the British were unwilling to see their ally accept the offers before they had had one last attempt to drive the Germans away from the North Sea coast of Belgium.

On 20 September a new assault, with the help of Plumer's 2nd Army, achieved a four-mile breakthrough on either side of the Menin road. This success, minor as it was, encouraged Haig to continue the fight into October and November 1917, hoping to take Passchendaele village itself. To achieve this Haig decided to use his best strike troops – Australians and New Zealanders. Their target was to take the village by 12 October, after which the Canadians and the Cavalry Corps would push on to the railway junction at Roulers and cut the Germans off from the coast. It sounded easy but the condition of the ground made it simply impossible.

Two British divisions – 49th and 66th – were earmarked to carry out preliminary work for the Australians. Unfortunately, on 10 October catastrophe struck the 66th. It was an inexperienced division which had not been properly briefed about its task. It arrived late, having spent nearly 24 hours on the march, without food or water. The covering barrage for the 66th was far too far forward and had to be ordered back. But the gunners were out of touch with the front line and as they brought back their barrage it struck the unlucky 66th, cutting the division to pieces and inflicting heavy casualties. The Australians had witnessed what had happened and their commander, Birdwood, complained to GHQ that he had just seen British soldiers wiped out by their own gunners. But the matter was hushed up.

Haig was confident that the Australians could achieve their mission, which was to take Passchendaele village. 'The New Zealand and Australian 3rd Division are to put the Australian flag in the church there,' he told his wife. But there were no flags and no celebrations; the attack was a disaster, with the Australians suffering 60 per cent casualties. Even Haig was prepared to admit that the ground now was 'quite impossible'. But the battle went on. Next it was the turn of the Canadians. But over half of their guns were underwater or clogged with mud or just 'missing', presumed submerged. Lieutenant-Colonel Alanbrooke – later of Second World War fame – attended one of Haig's briefings for the Canadians and could hardly believe his ears. Haig spoke as if the attack were taking place in high summer up a wide, dusty road with the enemy in retreat.

The Canadian Prime Minister Sir Robert Borden was so furious at what the Canadians had to endure that at one meeting of the Imperial War Cabinet he took Lloyd George by the lapels and shook him in a fury. Apparently, as a result of inaccurate orders, two companies of the Canadians had been positioned 100 yards ahead of the artillery barrage and as it was advanced both were blown to pieces by the British guns. Then the Canadian survivors, running back from the slaughter ahead, were attacked in error by two British companies supposedly supporting them. As an example of 'friendly fire' it was in a class of its own.

The capture of the village of Passchendaele on 4 November by the Canadians provided a suitable way of ending the battle. It had been a victory, all the communiqués contained the word. Ground had been gained and many casualties inflicted on the enemy. Admittedly, British casualties had been high – in truth closer to 350,000 than to the 238,000 given by the Official History. But what of the enemy? At the outset Haig had known that he had no men to spare, but that had not stopped him spending another third of a million of them even when he had heard that Britain's manpower was at bedrock. What had it all been for? Politically, of course, there had been targets unknown to the fighting man. But the Belgian coast had not been taken by the British, nor the German flank turned. And Germany was not driven by her losses to seek a peace on terms favourable to Britain. In fact, the Germans had lost far fewer men than the British – as few as 200,000 perhaps – in an operation that was supposed to sap their will to continue. All Haig had done was to demonstrate his – and Britain's – incapacity to win the war. Britain would now have to 'sit tight and wait for the Americans' to redress the balance on the Western Front.

30

Ludendorff's Offensive 1918

Victory against Russia on the Eastern Front in 1917 gave the German High Command the opportunity to transport nearly a million extra soldiers to the Western Front where, for the first time in the war, they would hold a numerical advantage over the Anglo-French forces. But by 1918 the Germans were convinced that even a victory over the French army, which had been unsettled by mutinies during 1917, would not persuade Britain to sue for peace. Only a decisive victory over the British army would give Germany the chance of victory before American troops arrived in such numbers as to swing the pendulum back to the allied side. As a result, General von Ludendorff planned a gigantic offensive against the already depleted British 5th Army, commanded by General Sir Hubert Gough, between the rivers Oise and Sambre, at the point where the British and French armies joined. Ludendorff's planning was excellent. There were strong reasons to suggest that the 5th Army might succumb to a sudden 'blitzkrieg' attack, prefaced by a short but overwhelming artillery bombardment and carried out by fast-moving elite 'shock' troops, using new tactics and advancing behind a 'creeping' barrage. The 5th Army was, in fact, the weakest of the British armies and covered the longest stretch of front. Once the 5th Army had been shattered and British troops forced to retreat in disorder, the Germans believed Britain would be more willing to entertain peace negotiations.

The Germans had been surprised at the resilience of the British army, which had suffered over 800,000 casualties in the previous twelve months and was nearly 70,000 men below establishment. Yet British resilience was more apparent than real. On closer analysis, combat exhaustion was at an unparalleled level during the winter of 1917–18 and, as more than one French general had observed in previous centuries, if the British had known how badly damaged they were they would have been defeated. Stubbornness and an unshakable will to win prompted Britain's generals and soldiers to go on fighting at whatever cost. Yet the fighting in the muddy slime of Passchendaele had filled the hospitals with thousands of men who were mentally rather than physically destroyed. And as the cry for reinforcements went up, in Britain the politicians became increasingly loath to allow Field Marshal Sir Douglas Haig, the British commander-in-chief, to squander British lives on further attritional battles. Prime Minister David Lloyd George held back more and more men of military age. Significantly, War Office figures for 1 January 1918 reveal that there were 38,225 officers and 607,403 fit and fully-trained soldiers in Britain, who could have gone to France and stiffened the British armies. Haig's armies were being starved just at the moment of their greatest danger.

At the start of 1918, Britain's real enemy was time. The American troops were arriving in France at a very slow rate, while the Germans were transporting ten whole divisions per month from Russia. Gradually, the German High Command – now the duo of Hindenburg and Ludendorff – were amassing such local superiority in Flanders that they would be able to launch an offensive against any point in the British line with a real chance of success. In fact, Ludendorff was planning a knock-out blow of Napoleonic finality. Three whole armies would attack the British 5th Army and the initial breakthrough would be spearheaded by new mobile squads of stormtroopers. To maximize the efficiency of the artillery barrage that would precede the attack, Colonel Bruchmüller, master of the 'creeping barrage', had been moved to the Western Front.

The storm burst at 4 a.m. on 21 March and the great offensive that was launched is sometimes known as the 'Kaiser' battle, because Kaiser Wilhelm II moved up to army headquarters to personally involve himself in what he supposed would be the war-winning victory. Along fifty miles of the British front line 6,000 German guns opened a five-hour barrage that was the biggest the world had ever known. Of the 100,000 British troops facing this German onslaught, no more than 2,500 were killed and

6,000 wounded, but it was not merely death and destruction that were the Germans' aim, but demoralization. In this they were very successful.

In contrast with the depressed and exhausted British, the German troops marched forward with supreme confidence, convinced that the end of the war was in sight. Inside the first sixty minutes General Gough had lost more than 30 per cent of 5th Army's infantry strength. In some places 'the British emerged with arms uplifted and knocking knees', while in others 'the fellows put up a superb show'. Yet, however well or badly the British fought, the result was the same: a complete collapse of the British front line in front of Péronne. British observers were in complete agreement as to what had happened. Captain Essame of the Northants Regiment described something he had never expected to see: a British rout.

Elsewhere, some regular officers were trying to stem the flight to the rear. Lieutenant-Colonel Sir Ian Colquhoun of the Scots Guards was marching up and down with pistol in hand like a Housemaster trying to stem a horde of unruly schoolboys. Not far away Regimental Sergeant Major Withers – known to his men as 'African Joe' from all his Boer War medals – was calling on the retreating soldiers to 'Be British! Be British!' and turn back to face the enemy. But panic took many forms. Some men panicked that day by running away, others by fighting when there was no hope. Many individual soldiers, even some units, took it upon themselves to fight to the death.

Lieutenant-Colonel J. H. Dimmer, VC, MC was a 'blood and thunder' soldier, who came from a 'blood and thunder' family. At the outbreak of war in 1914 he had been serving in West Africa, but he immediately sailed for home, joined his regiment and fought at the first battle of Ypres in 1914, where he won the Victoria Cross for outstanding courage in staying with his machine-gun and continuing fighting even though he had been wounded five times. On 21 March 1918, he was in command of his own battalion of Berkshire Territorials and his men were proud to be part of 'Colonel Dimmer's Battalion'. Dimmer only knew how to lead from the front. He therefore determined to lead his men in a counter-attack against the advancing Germans. But instead of concealing his officer's regalia, which made him an easy target, and leading his men from a crouching position, Dimmer insisted on mounting his horse so that everyone could take courage from his example. His officers tried to persuade him to dismount, but he was not a man for turning. With his groom riding by his side, he set off towards the Germans, with two companies of his men stumbling behind him. Soldiers from other regiments watched the amazing scene. One observer commented, 'We realized that the two horsemen were silhouetted against the skyline and we put up covering fire to protect them. But as soon as they reached the top, they were picked off and fell to the ground.' Dimmer was no El Cid, unfortunately. His death was futile. In the event, forty of his men were caught unnecessarily in the open and killed, and the rest of his battalion cracked and took to their heels.

In simple terms the British 5th Army had cracked and had run. For the first time, it was beginning to dawn on some of the stubborn English that they might actually be going to lose the war. On the other hand, the Germans were beginning to fall victim to their own success. They were undoubtedly motivated by the expectation of loot. Sergeant Friedrich Flohr explained: 'We knew that the Tommies had in their dug-outs all the good things that we hadn't – chocolate, coffee, corned beef, wine, spirits, cigars, cigarettes.'

Meanwhile, the authorities in England, who had held back reinforcements from their generals, now awoke to the fact that their action might be going to cost Britain the war. Immediately, replacements were rushed to France and in the space of a week over 100,000 new men arrived at the front. The German generals were drawing breath after the tremendous success of the 21 March offensive. Ludendorff had, in fact, already decided on a second assault, this time directed at the weakest point in the allied line, held by two Portuguese divisions, so desperate was the manpower situation. The British, displaying not for the first time in the war their irritating tendency to make fun of their friends, regarded their Portuguese allies as something of a joke. Even British generals called the Portuguese commander 'General Bumface' as he did not speak English and was otherwise old and apparently incompetent.

Just as the Allies were considering replacing the Portuguese with British troops the matter was taken out of their hands by the passage of events. First the Germans flooded the forward British and Portuguese positions with mustard gas, followed the next day by one of Bruchmüller's barrages, as violent and as sudden as an electric storm. While the divisions flanking the Portuguese hung on, their southern allies saw little reason to lay down their lives in a cause for which they cared little. Many of the Portuguese surrendered to the Germans even before Bruchmüller's barrage. Fearing the German shells behind them, some Portuguese ran towards advancing British troops, who fired at them as deserters. One British officer ordered machine-guns to be set up, specifically to shoot at the fleeing Portuguese. From whatever cause, within a matter of hours the 2nd Portuguese Division had been entirely wiped out.

But as the British were pressed back resistance began to stiffen. Where soldiers would not stand and fight willingly, some of the tougher breed of officer were offering them the stark choice: fight or die. Lieutenant-Colonel Seton Hutchison, leading a machine-gun battalion of the 33rd Division, was swept off the road by hundreds of retreating soldiers, claiming to have mysterious orders to retire. Hutchison was unimpressed. He commandeered an ambulance to take him back to divisional headquarters, gained permission to move his machine-guns forward, met opposition from a transport office when trying to requisition some lorries and persuaded the man to see sense by knocking him unconscious with his revolver. He then raced back to the crowd of panicking deserters and stopped them in their tracks by setting up eight machine-guns across their path. Any man who advanced a further step was immediately shot down and any officer who hesitated to do his duty was relieved of his command and arrested. Elsewhere, Brigadier-General Cozier was acting with equal ruthlessness. He it was who mowed down the fleeing Portuguese and later wrote of his experiences in a book entitled *Men I Killed*, the men in question being fleeing British soldiers rather than Germans. Even Ludendorff himself later recognized the effectiveness of the British methods in regaining control of a panicking army. Anything less decisive, he observed, and the war would have been won by the Germans.

As the German advance continued the morale of the two armies underwent a curious reversal. Success bred discontent in the German ranks, while disaster seemed, not for the first time, to steel the British resolve. Certainly, British morale was already improving before Haig issued his famous order of 11 April: 'There is no course open to us but to fight it out! Every position must be held to the last man; there must be no retirement. With our backs to the wall, and believing in the justice of our cause each one of us must fight to the end.'

On 14 April Australian troops in the British front line were assaulted by 'miles of infantry' advancing against them in a full frontal attack. What followed was nothing less than murder. The Australians held their fire until they had unmissable targets and then massed artillery simply mowed down the Germans at a range of less than a hundred yards. Four Australian machine-guns spent hours killing thousands of Germans who marched towards them like moths towards a lamp. The Germans simply lacked the mobility to exploit their breakthrough. With few tanks and having lost aerial superiority to the Royal Flying Corps, the German offensive, for all its massive potential, was petering out in the same way that every offensive since 1914 had – in bloody failure. Now they were measuring progress in hundreds of yards and not miles, while their losses in experienced troops could not be made good. Ludendorff's great gamble was beginning to fail. While the British had suffered over 300,000 casualties in less than a month, German losses had been as great if not greater. Moreover, although the offensive had begun with a panicky flight by the British front line it ended with 55 British divisions eventually repelling 109 German divisions.

Both sides learned valuable lessons from this vast struggle. For the British, the most important lesson was that to retreat does not mean to be beaten; for the Germans that to advance does not mean victory. Even at the lowest point of their fortunes, with their battle line broken and panic afflicting the troops, the average British soldier remained stubborn and phlegmatic. Things might be bad but the troops' pride in their race and their history enabled them to maintain their fighting spirit. And when their own commander-in-chief called on them to fight to the end, with their backs to the wall, they felt not inspired but angry. They fought the Germans to a standstill not because they were ordered to by their generals but because it was time to make a stand and put the Germans back in their place.

31

The Battle of Britain 1940

The German defeat in the battle of Britain was one of the turning points in the Second World War. Coming so soon after the defeat of France, it marked the first setback for Hitler's regime and one which had serious long-term consequences. Losses suffered by the Luftwaffe could not be easily made good and the loss of experienced pilots meant that the German air force was never again the potent force it had been in the early part of the war. The failure of the Luftwaffe in the battle of Britain was not merely a result of the activities of the heroic 'Few' but stemmed from fundamental weaknesses of aircraft design and military leadership. Hermann Goering involved his pilots in a battle that they simply could not win because he was more concerned with his personal reputation than with the welfare of the Third Reich.

When France surrendered in June 1940 everyone expected Britain to sue for peace. There seemed no reason to continue fighting once the military strength of the French army was gone. In fact, Hitler had no desire to fight Britain and was already planning an attack on the Soviet Union. But Britain did not surrender and the whole British attitude puzzled and perplexed the Führer. The opinion of the Commissionaire at the United Services Club was typical of Britain's reaction to the collapse of France: 'Anyhow, sir, we're in the Final, and it's to be played on the Home Ground.' Air Chief Marshal Dowding wrote, 'Thank God we're alone now.' The British people seemed to be displaying what has been called their 'sublime stupidity'.

By the beginning of July Hitler was beginning to realize that the British would not surrender and that he might have to invade

England by sea, not a prospect that the German High Command relished. The elimination of the French navy at Mers-el-Kebir by the Royal Navy on 3 July had shocked the Germans by its decisive and ruthless demonstration of British seapower. Now Hitler knew he was in for a fight. His response was a plan to invade England – Operation Sealion.

The Germans believed they would need 40 divisions to complete the conquest of Britain, and that by the third day 260,000 men, 40,000 vehicles and 60,000 horses would need to be ashore on the coasts of Kent and Sussex, which would require a logistics miracle. And the spectre of Britain's 800 torpedo boats and light craft breaking into the crowded troop convoys was one that caused the planners nightmares. There was simply no chance of a successful invasion unless the Royal Navy could be kept well away from the crossing points, and this would have to be done by the Luftwaffe. But before the German air force could go over to the job of attacking British shipping, air supremacy had to be achieved. The first task was to destroy the RAF, and Goering promised to achieve this in just four weeks – an estimate based on wishful thinking and poor intelligence. Frankly, the Luftwaffe was not strong enough to defeat both the RAF and the Royal Navy and the statistics were available to prove it. Only faulty analysis by Goering's planners could have overlooked this fact.

Figures for the comparative strengths of the Luftwaffe and the RAF at the start of the battle of Britain are notoriously difficult to give, as no two experts will ever agree. Suffice it to say that throughout the attritional fighting in August and September both sides were building new planes as fast as they could and replacing lost planes; they were also – with greater difficulty – replacing lost pilots and aircrew. At its strongest the RAF fielded 55 squadrons, and – at any one time – could put 666 aircraft into the air, out of a total strength of some 1,100 planes. Eighty per cent of Dowding's fighters were Hurricanes and Spitfires, the only British fighters that could face the best German planes, the Me.109s; the RAF's Blenheims, Defiants and Gladiators could only be used in a secondary capacity. On the German side, the three air fleets of the Luftwaffe fielded about 800 single-seat fighters and 300 heavy fighters, as well as 1,000 long-range bombers and 300 Stuka dive-bombers. Plane for plane the Germans had the advantage, with the excellent Bf109E outperforming the Spitfire and the slower Hurricane; but the quality of RAF pilots, drawn from fourteen countries including Nazi-occupied Poland and Czechoslovakia, was supreme. However, where the Germans suffered most was in their underestimation of RAF strength, and in their failure to realize the critically important role of British radar.

By 1940 radar had become a decisive arm of air defence, allowing the defenders to have enough warning of an approaching attack and its direction to allow their fighters to get airborne in time to meet the intruders. Once the enemy came in view the Royal Observer Corps came into play and German pilots were astounded to hear the air waves 'full of English voices' giving precise positions of the German planes. It was part of a far more sophisticated air-defence system than they had themselves, and its heart was Hugh Dowding's Operations Room in Bentley Priory, at Stanmore in Middlesex.

The battle began on 10 July, with German raids on British convoys in the Channel and on other naval targets, but the Germans were never able to achieve local air superiority, and their losses were always much higher than those of the British. The latter were often able to rescue pilots from their lost planes, whereas the German aircrew from destroyed planes were always either killed or captured.

On 1 August 1940 Hitler gave instructions for what was to be known as *Adler Tag* – Eagle Day – the start of the major air offensive. Eventually, bad weather postponed Eagle Day to 13 August. Yet on 12 August the Germans had scored a success against the British radar defence system, a success which should have pointed the way forward for them: an attack on the Isle of Wight radar station at Ventnor put the unit out of action for weeks. Ironically, Goering had just reached the conclusion that such raids were a waste of time, and so Britain's radar was saved. On 13–14 August the Germans flew 1,485 missions, losing 45 aircraft to the RAF's 13. At this time Goering was estimating RAF strength at just 300 serviceable fighters, whereas Dowding had 700. On 15 August the Germans flew 1,786 sorties in an attempt to crush Fighter Command once and for all, hitting airfields and communications sources, but their losses of 76 aircraft – exaggerated by a jubilant

RAF to 180 – were their largest of any day during the entire battle. Goering was losing so many senior air crew that he ordered that no more than one officer should fly in any plane. The fighting on 15 August was seen by many as decisive in the battle.

Goering now switched his single-seat fighters to the command of Kesselring's Luftflötte 2 in northeast France. Because of the short range of the German fighters Goering had concluded that he should concentrate the fight over the southern English counties, destroying RAF airfields where possible. The fighting was intense and dog-fights took place all across the skies of Kent, Sussex and Surrey.

In his search for a quick victory to allow Operation Sealion to go ahead Goering squandered German successes against the air-fields by shifting to a target that he believed the British would commit everything to defend: London. The background to this decisive and – from Germany's point of view – disastrous decision was that on 25 August British bombers had attacked Berlin. Although they had caused minimal damage, the blow to German prestige was enormous. How could the German people believe that the British were on the point of surrender if their bombers were in the sky over the German capital? In retaliation, Hitler ordered that London should be given the same treatment as Warsaw and Rotterdam. The shift in German bombing to London was the deci-sive moment of the battle of Britain. As time was to show – in 1943 and 1944 over Germany – victory in war could not be won by attacking urban areas in an attempt to lower civilian morale.

The four weeks between 15 August and 15 September saw the height of the attritional battle. In this period the RAF lost 493 planes with only 201 aircrew killed; the Germans lost 862 planes but with 1,132 aircrew killed. This haemorrhaging of trained and experi-enced pilots and crew could not be sustained indefinitely. Daylight raids on London were launched regularly in early September but though they caused much damage and heavy civilian casualties, they did nothing to reduce Britain's war potential. The Blitz had begun – but the martyrdom of London was to save the whole coun-try; as one commentator observed: 'The attraction of London was the German Air Force's undoing. Like an indestructible sponge it absorbed punishment and diverted what might have been the death blow from the sorely tried organism of defence.'

On 10 September Hitler decided to postpone Operation Sealion for seven days as no victory in the air was in sight. On 15 September, with just two days to go before the deadline, Kesselring launched a series of heavy raids, but in intense fighting he suffered losses of over 60 planes. That day – eventually chosen as 'Battle of Britain' day – was not perhaps as decisive as 15 August, yet it was enough to convince Hitler that the air war over Britain could not now be won. RAF bombers had reinforced that conclusion by raiding the German invasion ports and destroying 200 landing craft. By now Hitler had lost all faith in Goering's air offensive and postponed Operation Sealion again – this time indefinitely.

The Luftwaffe continued to strike London for twenty-three consecutive days in daylight, but their casualties were becoming prohibitive. By October they had lost 1733 planes to a RAF figure of 915, and it was clear that the air war had been lost. British factories were producing aircraft three times as fast as the Germans, and though it was the courage of the pilots that actually achieved victory in the air, the battle of Britain was a triumph for thousands of land-based personnel: air controllers, radar operators, engineers, ground crew and factory workers. If Churchill overlooked this when he said, 'Never in the field of human conflict has so much been owed by so many to so few', he was only reflecting the public view that, as in 1914–18, the British flyers were the heroes, the 'knights of the sky'.

The Germans lost the battle of Britain and, in the eyes of some Germans, the consequences for Germany were already fatal. General Werner Kreipe claimed: 'Though the air battles over England were perhaps a triumph of skill and bravery so far as the German air crews were concerned, from the strategic point of view it was a failure, and contributed to our ultimate defeat.' The RAF had so blunted German air power that never again in the war did the Luftwaffe achieve superiority or even parity with the British and Americans in the west.

32

The Battle of El Alamein 1942

On 28 June 1942 the British armies in North Africa stood on the brink of total defeat. In the words of General Sir Alan Brooke, 'The Middle East situation is about as unhealthy as it can be, and I do not very well see how it can end.' Rommel's Afrika Korps had just taken Tobruk and driven the British 8th Army back 750 miles from the frontiers of Libya to a line not two hours' drive from Alexandria and the Nile Delta. In Cairo a pall of smoke rose from the British embassy as records and secret documents were burned. In Alexandria Barclays Bank paid out one million pounds in a single day as customers panicked and fled, their cars clogging the roads to the east. Britain was facing a defeat that would rank with the most disastrous in her history, with the certain loss of Egypt and her vast military base there, as well as that of the Suez Canal, her lifeline to the east. But more than that, in the context of the war itself, the consequences for the Allies of a British collapse would have been to allow a refuelled and resupplied Rommel to drive on to occupy the Middle East with its tremendous oil resources, and to link up with German forces which were on the point of taking Rostov and pushing south into the Caucasus, undermining the Soviet Union's southern front. Command of the Red Sea would have enabled Italian and German warships and submarines to threaten Allied links with the Far East and open up the possibility of Germany 'joining hands' with the Japanese in the Indian Ocean. Nor was this simply a 'Domesday scenario'. It was a part of Hitler's long-term strategical plan, and if Rommel could drive the British from their hastily erected defences at El Alamein there was nothing left to prevent him achieving it.

The British 8th Army, commanded by General Sir Claude Auchinleck, were dug in on the 40-mile-wide 'Alamein Line' stretching from the coastal village of El Alamein to the Qattara Depression, just 60 miles west of the Nile. To the British soldiers at Alamein there was no defensive line, just open, seemingly limitless desert; but Auchinleck was with them, sharing their hardships and their rations. It was an inhospitable place, as General Bayerlein of the Afrika Korps describes: 'A stony, waterless desert where bleak outcrops of dry rock alternated with stretches of sand sparsely clotted with camel scrub beneath the pitiless African sun – such was the Alamein front in July of 1942.'

Yet here the British 'Desert Rats' turned on Rommel's Afrika Korps and in prolonged fighting during July 1942 inflicted a decisive check on the German advance. Although British casualties were heavier than Rommel's, there can be no doubt that, if there was a single turning point in the whole Desert War, it was this vital but unheralded 'grapple' that saved Egypt. Auchinleck had absorbed punishment from a reinforced Afrika Korps and had 'wasted' Rommel's enormous materiel gains from his capture of Tobruk. The Afrika Korps that Montgomery would later face had had its wings clipped. But Churchill, for one, refused to see it that way. He wanted a new commander and appointed General Harold Alexander to replace Auchinleck as overall Middle Eastern commander and Lieutenant-General Bernard Law Montgomery to lead the 8th Army in place of Ritchie. Montgomery's orders were simple: 'Go down to the desert and defeat Rommel.' General Montgomery was not Churchill's original choice to succeed Ritchie, but when General 'Strafer' Gott was killed in a plane crash, 'Monty' got the job on Alexander's recommendation.

The Germans had no intention of letting the new man settle in. On 31 August Rommel attacked the 8th Army around the Alam Halfa Ridge, but in a hard-fought, drawn battle the German offensive was held. Rommel's health now collapsed and he was taken to Austria for treatment, leaving the ailing General Georg von Stumme in charge of German forces. Montgomery meanwhile set about stamping his authority on the 8th Army. He brought his own peculiar sense of humour to the task, telling both officers and men that they would soon 'knock the enemy for six, right out of Africa', and that their job was to kill Germans, 'even the padres – one per weekday and two on Sundays.' But his humour was measured; he could be prickly and dictatorial. Of him it was said, 'In defeat, indomitable; in victory, insufferable.' He was helped by the sort of massive reinforcement in men and materiel for which Auchinleck would have given his eye-teeth.

By October, the 8th Army stood at 9 infantry and 3 armoured divisions, totalling 200,000 men, with over 1,100 tanks – including American Grants and Shermans with 75 mm guns, a match for the Panzer Mark IV tank – and strong artillery, which Montgomery was going to use as if preparing for one of Haig's vast World War One setpieces. Against this von Stumme could oppose about 96,000 men – half German and half Italian units with a stiffening of German NCOs – as well as 500 tanks, of which only half were German and the rest relatively weak Italian models. On paper, everything favoured Montgomery, who had a 2 to 1 advantage in men and 3 to 1 in materiel, as well as air supremacy.

On the night of 23 October 1942 the first stage of Montgomery's plan – Operation Lightfoot – began with a powerful bombardment from 900 heavy and medium guns, taking the enemy completely by surprise. The British gunners were soon deafened by the roar of their own pieces, their thick gloves burned away by the heat of the barrels. Rommel was convalescing in Austria at the time and the unfortunate von Stumme – rushing to the front and ambushed by an Australian patrol – succumbed to a heart attack.

Under cover of the artillery two British infantry strikes were made: in the north four divisions of Leese's XXX Corps struck along the coast from El Alamein to tear corridors through enemy minefields towards Kidney Ridge and over the Miteiriya Ridge, opening the way for Gatehouse's 10th Armoured Division from Lumsden's X Corps; further south, Horrocks' XIII Corps made two thrusts: one east of Jebel Kalakh and the other towards Himeimat. This southern thrust was designed to mislead the Germans into thinking it was the main strike and to persuade them to commit part of their armour away from the main thrust in the north. Captain Grant Murray described the advance in the darkness: 'Line upon line of steel-helmeted figures, with rifles at the high port, bayonets catching in the moonlight . . . gave us the thumbs-up sign.

We watched them plod on towards the enemy lines which were by this time shrouded in smoke.'

Everywhere the British troops were held up by the depth of Rommel's minefields – his 'Devil's gardens' of 500,000 anti-tank and anti-personnel mines – which were up to five miles deep. And the German artillery, notably their 88 mm guns, took a heavy toll of the British armour. Major John Larkin saw 27 British tanks 'go up in sheets of flame one by one, just as if someone had lit the candles on a birthday cake'. By 25 October Rommel had reluctantly returned from Austria to take command of his Afrika Korps, admitting 'there are no more laurels to be earned in Africa'. Short of tanks and fuel and subject to constant bombing and strafing from the RAF, the best he could hope for was to hold the British in a clinch. But in this kind of attritional struggle he knew he must lose in the long run.

On 31 October Montgomery, undeterred by his lack of progress so far, launched the second phase of the operation, code-named 'Supercharge', directed towards Tel el Aqqaqir, that overran the Italian Trento Division and punched holes in the German defences, allowing British armour to break out into open desert behind the German lines. Rommel, now with just 35 tanks operational and most of his vehicles short of fuel, was faced with complete disaster. Rejecting Hitler's directive to 'stand and die' he ordered a general withdrawal on the night of 4/5 November, abandoning most of his Italian troops. What began as a strategic withdrawal to regroup eventually became a full retreat for nearly 1,500 miles, as the 8th Army raced the Afrika Korps all the way back to Tunisia.

Four of Germany's best divisions and eight Italian ones had been destroyed in the battle, and the Axis troops had suffered 20,000 battle casualties, with a further 30,000 prisoners. Almost the entire Axis tank strength had been eliminated, along with 1,000 guns. The 8th Army had suffered heavy losses themselves: 13,500 battle casualties, 500 tanks and over 100 guns, for the battle had been fought with unprecedented ferocity, the British knowing that defeat would have cost them Egypt and the Suez Canal. When news of Montgomery's victory reached Britain, Churchill ordered the church bells to be rung – not as they once would have been, to signal invasion – but to celebrate Britain's greatest victory of the war. In Churchill's words, 'Before Alamein we never had a victory. After Alamein we never had a defeat.' Churchill was unfair, as usual, in his generalization. Without Auchinleck's defensive victory at the first battle of El Alamein there would have been no second battle of El Alamein to give Montgomery his greatest triumph.

33

The Battle of Arnhem 1944

Like Dunkirk, Arnhem was one of the heroic defeats Britain suffered in the Second World War, much beloved of British film producers. As a result, myth-makers have tended to conceal from the British people what a deplorable series of errors and professional incompetence surround Operation 'Market Garden'.

The opening of the Second Front after the Allied landings in Normandy in June 1944 did not bring the swift end to the Second World War that many people had expected. The fighting in Normandy and across France to the German border was some of the most ferocious of the entire war, and with the Allies' determination to impose 'unconditional surrender' on the Germans it was clear that this could not be achieved without a full invasion of Germany and an occupation of Berlin. 21st Army group commander General Montgomery proposed a single deep thrust through the German defences and a crossing of the Rhine from Holland, prior to a descent into the German industrial heartland of the Ruhr. As a result, Operation 'Market Garden' was born. To achieve this Montgomery planned to use Lieutenant-General Sir Frederick Browning's 1st Airborne Corps to capture three decisive bridges: the first across the Waal would be taken by US 82nd Airborne Division under General Maxwell Taylor; the next, across the Maas at Nijmegen, was earmarked for the US 101st under General Gavin; and the last, at Arnhem, would be captured and held by the British 1st Airborne Division, commanded by General Roy Urquhart. Once captured, the bridge at Arnhem had to be held by the British paratroops for two days while British XXX Corps under General Horrocks drove their tanks up the single narrow road from

Nijmegen. It was a tight plan that depended on almost everything going right. In the event, almost everything went wrong.

The first problem that influenced everything else was that there were not enough American transport aircraft available to shift the entire British airborne contingent in one day – nor even in two days, but in three! The American airborne divisions were both being delivered in one day – the 101st at Eindhoven and the 82nd at Nijmegen – but the British and Poles at Arnhem would take three days. With surprise gone, many Poles were killed unnecessarily as the Germans were waiting for their drop on the third day. Secondly, not only would the British arrive in three drops but they could not be dropped closer to their objective – the bridge at Arnhem – than about eight miles and in the middle of a swarm of enemy troops and heavy armour at that. As it turned out, planning went so wrong that the paratroops would have to fight their way through to Arnhem bridge, then hold it for three times as long as planned, completely without air support and all the time unable to communicate with their disparate parts through radio insufficiency. It was a grim story of errors which might have been anticipated or rectified in advance. In the first place, what were German Panzer troops doing at the drop site anyway? At least one British officer knew the answer to this but he was sent on sick leave when he tried to pass on his knowledge to his superiors. Major Brian Urquhart, an Intelligence Officer on General Browning's staff, had evidence that two Panzer divisions – 9th (Hohenstaufen) and 10th (Frundsberg) – were resting and reforming near Arnhem. Urquhart had ordered a photo reconnaissance over the area on 15 September and had got what he wanted – photographic evidence that modern German tanks were just eight miles from the landing area selected for 1st Airborne. But this was not the sort of news that the men at the top wanted to hear. As a result, they simply pretended it was not true and carried on regardless. It was arranged that a senior medical officer should meet Urquhart and arrange for him to be sent on sick leave due to his 'nervous strain and exhaustion'. Too much was riding on 'Market Garden' for it to be cancelled at this stage, whatever intelligence might come up with to cast doubt on it.

The second question that could be asked was: Why were the British paratroopers dropped so far from the bridge? As it happened the commander of the 1st Airborne Division was also called Urquhart – no relation of the Intelligence Officer (above) – and was a new appointment. The dropping zones for his men were not chosen by him but were chosen because it was supposed that the area to the south of Arnhem was too low-lying and marshy and quite unsuitable for glider landings. As a result, the areas chosen were in woods north of the city and heathland to the west, between five and eight miles away from the Rhine bridge. Urquhart tried to get this changed but he was overruled. He had been supported in this by the Polish commander, General Sosabowski, who was highly critical of the air plan and believed it would fail because the British were abandoning surprise in favour of feeding in troops piecemeal.

A further question needs to be asked. Why was it so difficult for the British troops to communicate with each other at Arnhem? The answer is that their radios were faulty. By 1944 Britain's airborne troops operated three different radio strengths: the standard unit – the '19' – with a range of twelve miles was too large to be carried by a soldier and needed a jeep for transport; the '22' was smaller, though still needed a jeep and had a range of just six miles; the smallest set was the '68' and was portable, but had a range of just three miles. Size being a priority, most of the sets with 1st Airborne were the '68s'. But as the British paratroopers were dropped in a zone which covered a large area most of them were out of radio range of each other. Even before the 1st Airborne Division left Britain it was known that there would be a virtual communications blackout for much of the first day, or even longer if units met heavy opposition or failed to assemble quickly. In an attempt to maintain contact with his various units, Major-General Urquhart eventually took a jeep and personally delivered his orders. Unfortunately, he was forced to shelter with a Dutch family as German troops surrounded their house. He was missing for 36 hours, part of which time he was sheltering in their attic.

The first air drop took place on 17 September, when Brigadier Lathbury arrived on schedule near Arnhem with his 1st Parachute Brigade. Part of this under Lieutenant-Colonel John Frost, mainly men of 2 Para, fought their way into Arnhem and took possession of one end of the bridge road. Frost's men were welcomed as liberators by the Dutch population, receiving flowers and kisses, but it soon became apparent to everyone that this was no picnic. The first problem they faced tested the etiquette of the officers. They had to take possession – with or without permission – of the houses near the bridge. At the house of the Kneists, one officer showed such good manners that he set up his machine gun out on the pavement rather than disturb the many old people inside. But this sort of thing could not last long. Soon the Dutch householders were sheltering in the cellars while the German tanks systematically blew their houses to pieces above their heads. The curious old-world charm of British officers like Major Tatham-Warter, leading his men with a rolled umbrella, could not disguise for long that these British paratroopers were the toughest of men, unwilling to sacrifice their positions whatever the Germans brought against them. And now commenced an epic battle for the control of the bridge, with Frost's 750 assorted troops outnumbered many times over by an entire Panzer division, equipped with the latest tanks. All eyes that were not watching the Germans were gazing across the river for a sight of XXX Corps' tanks which were supposed to arrive in two days. But the Guards Armoured Division of XXX Corps under General Alan Adair found it impossible to progress beyond Nijmegen until Gavin's 101st had taken the bridge against strong opposition.

At Arnhem the first day's fighting on the bridge began with what appeared to be a celebratory procession of 22 armoured cars and half-tracks, packed with 9th Divisions best troops, under the command of one of their divisional heroes, Hauptsturmführer Victor Graebner, complete with his recently awarded Knight's Cross. But the Germans had grossly underestimated the task ahead and as they crossed the bridge they were met by a torrent of anti-tank and machine-gun fire from Frost's men, during which Graebner was shot dead and virtually his whole unit destroyed. It was a massacre rather than a battle. Inside the houses the British were still living the surreal experience of maintaining the niceties with the aged Dutch inhabitants, while out front they were slaughtering German soldiers. In one house the British were asked 'Please don't fire from here; it's my husband's favourite room.' Meanwhile, two German tanks had returned to the bridge and were forcing their way through the smouldering wrecks littering the road, opening a path for the infantry behind them. The fighting was short and sharp. Again the anti-tank gunners were successful, leaving two more wrecks on the bridge road.

The Germans faced a dilemma. They would have liked to take their time destroying the British positions by the bridge at Arnhem but they needed to break through quickly to send reinforcements to Nijmegen where a tremendous battle was raging, involving British XXX Corps' tanks. Nevertheless, their anxiety to break through had left the bridge littered and blocked, with so many vehicles burning that the road surface was melting. On the second day of fighting they approached the problem more systematically.

Rather than use infantry against the entrenched British para-troopers, the Germans concentrated on destroying the buildings that sheltered them, blowing them to pieces with artillery and tank bombardment. Soon most of the houses were burning from phosphorus shells. Even Tiger tanks with 88-mm guns were called into action. Frost's command was reduced to just two anti-tank guns and scarcely any ammunition. The houses where 2 Para sheltered were brimming over with hundreds of their wounded comrades. It was only a matter of time before the Germans would overrun them. One of the men there described the scene at nightfall on the third day: 'The area around the bridge was becoming a sea of flame. The roar and crackle of flaming buildings and dancing shadows cast by the flames was like looking into Dante's inferno.'

Frost was fitfully in contact with Divisional HQ. When he was able to speak he called for reinforcements, ammunition and food. Urquhart knew he could offer nothing but the hope that XXX Corps would arrive in time. Both would have been crushed had they known that even as they spoke Nijmegen bridge was still in German hands. There was no hope of Adair's tanks reaching them yet. Up until the third day Frost, already known to the Germans as the 'mad Colonel', had led a charmed life but his luck ran out when a mortar bomb exploded nearby, injuring him in both legs.

By the fourth night, with their commander gone, 2 Para was reduced to less than a hundred men and almost out of ammunition when they were overrun by Germans and forced to surrender. They were not to realize until after the war, when they were liberated by

American troops of General Patton's 3rd Army, that their defence of Arnhem bridge had led directly to the fall of Nijmegen. But once across the Maas, Horrocks had decided not to make a desperate race to Arnhem to save them. The story of 'Too little too late' was part of another tradition. Ironically, it was the Americans who took the abandonment of Frost's men the hardest. Gavin was livid at the fate of his fellow-paratroopers and the GIs who liberated 2 Para's prisoners from a German POW camp in 1945 noted their red berets. As Frost later wrote, 'All ranks of this army would say, Arnhem. Aye. We'd have gotten through. Yes, sir. We'd have gotten through.' Frost reflected on this: 'I couldn't help believing that they would have.'

Elsewhere, Urquhart and most of the 1st Airborne troops – five paratroop and three glider-borne infantry battalions – had not even the grim satisfaction of heroic resistance that Frost's men had. They were pinned down in an ever decreasing perimeter around the Hartenstein Hotel, to the west of Arnhem. Here they held on until it became obvious that the bridge was lost and the survivors were evacuated across the Rhine on the night of 25/26 September.

General Montgomery's final comment on 'Market-Garden' that it had been nine-tenths a success is an odd one. The battle at Arnhem saw the virtual destruction of the British 1st Airborne Division. Of the 11,920 British and Polish airborne troops who landed at Arnhem, 1,485 died and 6,525 were taken prisoner, which comprised casualties of 67 per cent. Yet few failures in British history were so heroic as John Frost's defence of the bridge at Arnhem.

34

The Battles of
Kohima-Imphal 1944

Eastern India had been one of the targets for the Japanese expansion in south-east Asia since 1942 but it was felt by the Japanese High Command that an overland campaign from Upper Burma would be risky because of the almost impassable terrain. However, the success of Orde Wingate's 'Chindits' showed the Japanese what could be achieved in these jungle areas and, as Japan was suffering defeat after defeat in the Pacific at the hands of the American Navy, they concluded that victory in India would lift morale and might strike at the 'Achilles' heel' of the entire Allied war effort in south-east Asia. They believed that if the British lost control of north-east India it would severely hamper the operations against them in Burma by General Slim's 14th Army and, as a result, in 1944 they decided to instigate a 'March on Delhi'.

The Japanese plan for the invasion of India was designed to divide the strength of the British forces on the Arakan front along the Indo-Burmese border. Japan would then be able to occupy East Bengal by driving through the town of Chittagong. The second phase of this operation would involve the capture of the British base at Imphal and the railway junction at Dimapur after the British commander-in-chief General Slim had been forced to withdraw his reserves from there to support his position in Arakan. For this ambitious plan the Japanese assembled two armies in Burma, totalling 200,000 men. The assault in Arakan was to be led by the fanatical General Tanahashi, who concentrated his attack on the main British supply base at Sinzweya, known as the 'Admin Box'. At Sinzweya the Japanese attackers, supported by airstrikes from Zero fighter-bombers, furiously assaulted the Admin Box, where

General Messervy and his garrison were holding out. Yet in spite of everything the Japanese could throw at them, the defenders not only held them off but in hand-to-hand encounters British, Indian, and Ghurka soldiers established a moral superiority over the Japanese. By 11 February, the Admin Box had survived five days and nights of constant attacks. The decisive day was 17 February, the most significant day in the whole Burma war, when the Japanese Imperial Army admitted defeat for the first time and began to fall back. Out of General Sakuri's 7,000 assault troops, 5,000 died in the attack on the Admin Box. British casualties were 500 dead and 1,500 wounded. Significantly, for the first time Japanese prisoners were taken alive. The 14th Army had proved that the Japanese were not invincible.

For the second part of the Japanese plan, 100,000 of their best troops crossed the Chindwin River and attacked Kohima and Imphal. These troops were the best available to Japan and had been withdrawn from other fields of action throughout south-east Asia. The main target for the Japanese was the rail head at Dimapur, set up by the British in the jungle in 1942. On 17 March, the advance troops of the Japanese arrived around Kohima, thereby for the first time reaching Indian soil. Two Japanese divisions were given the order to advance 'through the hills like a ball of fire' and seize Imphal. They were given few supplies and told that everything they would need would be in Imphal. However, this was a battle that would be fought on the ground but won in the air. Air superiority allowed the RAF to bring out 13,000 casualties of the fighting and take in masses of food and other supplies. Cigarettes – 43 million of them – helped maintain morale, as well as the 12,000 sacks of mail taken in by the Dakotas. In contrast, the Japanese received nothing from outside and had to subsist on the barest diet.

Meanwhile, eighty miles from Imphal, the British outpost of Kohima, set among the hills 5,000 feet above sea level, was about to take centre stage for sixteen days and nights. At the centre of its defences was the District Commissioner's bungalow, his gardens and his tennis court. In the battle that followed these areas were to be fought over with incredible ferocity. Kohima, in fact, was vital to the defence of Dimapur, which had no garrison and, had the Japanese won, would have opened the way to their control of the giant American air bases inside the Indian border, which kept Chiang Kai-Shek and his Nationalist forces supplied in China.

The British garrison at Kohima numbered just 1,000 troops, which were about to be attacked by 15,000 of Japan's best soldiers. Even worse, Dimapur was defended by fewer than 500 men. If Kohima fell, then Dimapur was doomed. Logically, the Japanese should have bypassed Kohima – which was irrelevant in itself – and gone on to capture the rail junction at Dimapur. However, the Japanese commander in the attack on Kohima, Major-General Sato, was an inflexible martinet of the old school. He had been given orders to capture Kohima and that – and that alone – was what he was determined to do. Fortunately for the Allies, Sato burned himself out attacking Kohima. On 4 April Kohima was reinforced by the 4th Battalion of the Royal West Kents and by Indian troops so that its garrison rose to 3,500. In spite of this useful acquisition of troops, Kohima's survival depended on the RAF maintaining absolute air mastery. As a result, the defenders of Kohima could be supplied with everything from the air. The Japanese, on the other hand, had no airborne supplies and soon suffered desperate shortages of every kind. The fighting was so intense that much of it centred around the Commissioner's bungalow and for a while each side held one corner of the tennis court, constantly bombarding each other with grenades. For sixteen days the siege of Kohima continued until at last further British reinforcements reached the outpost on 18 April. Two days later further troops from 2nd Division appeared and drove the Japanese back. Even then it was not until a tank was manhandled onto the tennis court that the Japanese could be blasted out of their fortified positions. Throughout the battle the Japanese showed fanatical courage and it was not until 13 May that the last Japanese were driven away from the area of Kohima. None surrendered but the jungle around the outpost was filled with the reeking, unburied bodies of Japanese soldiers who had no way out of the struggle, except through victory or death. While the RAF evacuated thousands of British wounded the Japanese fought and died without hope of relief, eking out an existence on grass and slugs.

Around Imphal the Japanese 15th Division fought with the fury of despair but were gradually overwhelmed by Allied air superiority. Soon the Japanese were in full retreat, devoid of food, medicine and ammunition. Thousands of them died unnoticed in the jungle. Of the Japanese armies that invaded India 50,000 were counted as corpses on the battlefield. How many died in the jungle we will never know. The victory of Slim's 14th Army, sometimes known as the 'forgotten army', was one of the greatest unsung episodes of British military history. British troops, fighting in unaccustomed jungle conditions, succeeded in destroying two major Japanese armies and inflicting on Japan the greatest land defeat it suffered in the Second World War.

35

The Battle of
Goose Green 1982

The invasion of the Falkland Islands in April 1982 had been designed to bolster a fragile and unpopular junta in Argentina and was based on the belief that the British did not care enough about their far-flung colonies to go to war for them. Certainly, Treasury cutbacks in Britain had reduced the armed services to the point where an operation of the kind eventually launched in the South Atlantic went beyond the acceptable risk levels associated with military operations. Nevertheless, once the British Task Force sailed south its determination could not be questioned. But the Conservative government of Margaret Thatcher was aware of the risks that were being taken and needed an early victory to maintain public support for the war. Naval losses were so heavy at the outset that once a military landing had been made at San Carlos, the pressure was on for a propaganda victory.

There was an obvious target: the Argentinian garrison at Darwin-Goose Green, thirteen miles south of San Carlos. Yet the professional soldiers on the ground were unhappy about fighting political battles. They saw Goose Green as irrelevant to the main target, which was the capital, Port Stanley. As acting ground commander, Brigadier Julian Thompson tried to explain that, once Port Stanley fell, the defenders of Goose Green would be left with no alternative but to surrender anyway. Thompson would have preferred just to mask Darwin-Goose Green with a covering force to prevent any danger of an Argentinian flank attack when the main force set out for Port Stanley, but the politicians needed their tabloid headlines and so Goose Green had to be taken.

Seven thousand miles away in Britain the landing at San Carlos had excited the War Cabinet and misled them into thinking that the war was as good as over. They had briefed the press and given the impression that good news on the military front was imminent, perhaps even the fall of Port Stanley itself. The word from Mrs Thatcher via her Press Secretary, Bernard Ingham, was that 'We're not going to fiddle around.' This was typical of political rather than military jargon and paid no regard whatsoever to the logistical problems faced by the troops at San Carlos.

The Chiefs of Staff in Britain believed that a successful land engagement was a valuable means of establishing a psychological superiority over the Argentinians. They claimed that the enemy was weak and would present only token resistance. Yet did the Chiefs of Staff and the War Cabinet have any idea of the real situation at San Carlos? Under constant air raids as they were, the men at the front knew that the Argentinians were not as weak as was popularly supposed.

On 26 May, Brigadier Thompson received a direct order from London to attack Goose Green. This decision, as it transpired, was based on faulty intelligence reports that Goose Green was held by just one weak Argentinian battalion or about 400 men so that 2 Para – 450 men strong under Colonel 'H' Jones – would be easily strong enough to take the settlement, supported as it would be by the naval gunnery of HMS *Arrow*. However, British intelligence was wrong about the Argentine garrison, which, in fact, consisted of over 1,000 men as well as a substantial number of non-combatants, including air force personnel. The British were opting for a straightforward infantry action, in which they relied on their superior tactics and leadership to offset the Argentinian advantage in numbers and position. Surprisingly, the opportunity was not taken to reinforce 2 Para in view of the importance being placed on the battle as a 'make or break' encounter.

General Menéndez, the Argentinian commander in the Falklands, brought in reinforcements to Goose Green once it was obvious that the British intended to attack it. Incredibly, a BBC report announced that 2 Para was within five miles of the settlement but, in spite of the fact that it was true, the Argentinians regarded it as a bluff. They assumed that nobody in wartime could possibly make such a mistake. Colonel Jones was so infuriated by the broadcast that he vowed to sue the Defence Secretary at least on his return to Britain. The garrison at Goose Green, commanded by Lieutenant-Colonel Italo Piaggi, amounted to about 1,000 fighting men, of whom some were good quality troops, well armed and well entrenched, though others were conscripts or air force personnel with no infantry experience. In general they were well equipped and their boots were far better than the British boots, which leaked. 2 Para were now heading for an encounter with an enemy that outnumbered them by at least two to one.

Brigadier Thompson's plan for the operation involved 2 Para under 'H' Jones marching south from its position at Sussex Mountain. Shortages of helicopters meant that everything the men needed would have to be carried; therefore rations were limited to two days', and some heavier equipment was left behind. Much reliance was placed on the support of naval gunnery but in the event the Arrow's firing was intermittent because of mechanical failure and its shells ineffective through sinking into the peaty surface. In the end, shorn of artillery support and – through poor weather – aerial support, the men triumphed through their sheer fighting qualities in hand-to-hand engagements. It was a 'soldier's battle' – a miniature Inkerman – with commanders forced to lead by example. Tragically, while trying to get his troops moving again, and fighting like a company commander with 'A' Company, Colonel 'H' Jones was killed by machine-gun fire. With the battalion commander dead, matters might have taken a serious turn for the worse but Major Chris Keeble took over and kept things moving smoothly.

Throughout the fighting the Argentinians received sporadic reinforcement by helicopter but the British paratroops were relentlessly clearing trench after trench with small-arms fire and grenades, and even at the point of the bayonet. In the confused fighting one incident occurred which was to sour relations between the soldiers on both sides for the rest of the war. With groups of Argentinians surrendering in some trenches while others fought on, a British officer approached one group which was showing a white flag, only to be shot with two of his men by another group of Argentinians. Believing these killings were the result of treachery, the British fought with a new bitterness. However, the nature of the fighting at Goose Green suggests that the 'fog of war' was really responsible.

An improvement in weather conditions allowed two Sea Harriers to leave the aircraft carriers and support 2 Para at Goose Green. Their bombing seemed to shatter the nerves of the Argentinians still fighting, and soon hundreds of them were flooding back to Goose Green, having abandoned their weapons. The imminence of victory inspired the men of 2 Para, without sleep for the third night, without rations and in the snow, but within hours of the first victory of the war. Keeble now decided to try to bluff the Argentinians into surrender. Unaware that they were under attack by such a small force, the Argentinians needed to be convinced that overwhelming strength was about to descend on them. As a result, two prisoners were sent in to negotiate with Piaggi and convince him that he was surrounded. Fortunately, Piaggi saw reason. First, 250 Air Force personnel surrendered, followed by over 800 soldiers. Both sides exaggerated the casualties they had inflicted. The men of 2 Para believed they had killed 250 of the Argentinians but this is probably too high a figure; 100–150 seems closer to the truth, along with perhaps 100 men wounded. For its own numbers, 2 Para suffered 18 killed and 35 wounded, including 'H' Jones and eleven other officers and NCOs dead. It was the leadership of men like this that brought victory in this small but vicious battle. Appropriately, Colonel 'H' Jones was awarded a posthumous Victoria Cross for his part in the battle of Goose Green. Victory had been won by the sheer professionalism of 2 Para, yet with hindsight it seems incredible that Britain was willing to fight her first battle on the Falklands with such a small infantry force. There were more men available and the decision should have been taken that if they were going to have to fight at Goose Green they had better make sure that they won. To rely on such a small attacking force was to run the risk of a military setback which could have sent civilian morale plummeting in Britain. A British defeat might even have intensified moves to force both sides to agree to a ceasefire. The attack on Goose Green was an example of the sort of 'backseat-driving' that had led to disasters during the Second World War, and defeat would have called into question the whole strategy of sending an under-equipped expedition to the tip of South America in pursuit of aims that a post-colonial Britain should have outgrown. In the end the politicians relied on the heroism and superb fighting qualities of British troops to see them through and, as usual throughout history, the British soldier did not let them down.

Index

183